THE
HEART OF DAVID
JOURNAL

Leadings With Vision, Passion and Wisdom

VOLUME 3

By David Mayorga

Edited by Emily Rose King

Published by

SHABAR PUBLICATIONS
www.shabarpublications.com

CONTENTS

Volume 3

1

Created for Divine Order! – Part 1

"But when He saw the multitudes, He was moved with compassion for them, because they were weary and scattered, like sheep having no shepherd." (Matthew 9:36)

Check this out: As I was teaching on the Kingdom of God principles this past week, we were meditating upon the Father's true purpose for Jesus coming to earth. Holy Spirit arrested my heart with this thought, and I heard Him say to me, "David, I came to set everything in its rightful place: I came to fix what was broken; to heal that which was sick; to place people in their God-given calling since from the foundations of the world."

After hearing this from the Spirit within me, God took me to the verse I mentioned above. It is with this thought in mind that I am writing these notes.

When the Lord came to earth, He showed up with an agenda that was not His. It was a heavenly agenda, ordered by our heavenly Father, but administered to us by Jesus, His Son.

This heavenly agenda was a simple one: Reintroduce the kingdom of heaven on earth! That is what Jesus was all about, nothing else. Everything He did, His miracles, His teachings, His compassion, were all means to an end. Please understand that.

As you study the gospels, you will notice Jesus speaking through parables about the kingdom of God and its characteristics. Over and over again, Jesus made reference to life in the kingdom of God— its culture, its standards, its economy, etc.

Now here is where it gets interesting. When dealing with humanity, Jesus said this at one event, read on: **"Then Jesus went about all the cities and villages, teaching in their synagogues, preaching the gospel of the kingdom, and healing every sickness and every disease among the** people. But when He saw the multitudes, He was moved with compassion for them, because they were weary and scattered, like sheep having no shepherd. Then He said to His disciples, 'The harvest truly is plentiful, but the laborers are few. Therefore pray the Lord of the harvest to send out laborers into His harvest.'" (Matthew 9:35-38)

Jesus didn't feel compassion because they were hungry, or because they were wandering around having nothing better to do; Jesus saw what very few see today. He saw them like sheep having no shepherd!

This is the equivalent of a baby left by themselves by the side of the road with no one to tend to them! It is only a matter of time before this baby dies of starvation or is devoured by some wild animal.

Do you see why the Lord broke down? Do you see where true compassion is found? True compassion is found in the heart that realizes that an individual has no government, leader, or guidance of any sort in their lives— the odds of that person making it in life are very slim! Unless a shepherd comes to the aid of that sheep, that sheep will be eaten by wolves! Do you see it?

True compassion sees the root of the problem. True compassion knows and sees that unless the kingdom of God comes into a person, that individual will suffer all through life without guidance, without any spiritual support.

The lack of the kingdom of God in any individual, will be manifested in so many ugly and destructive ways!

2

Created for Divine Order! – Part 2

"And Jesus, walking by the Sea of Galilee, saw two brothers, Simon called Peter, and Andrew his brother, casting a net into the sea; for they were fishermen. Then He said to them, 'Follow Me, and I will make you fishers of men.' They immediately left their nets and followed Him." (Matthew 4:18-20)

Fishing in the Wrong Place!

I want to pick up our story here where Jesus shows up as He began to establish God's agenda on earth.

Apparently, Jesus is recruiting and is looking for a few good men that will follow Him, learn of Him, and are willing to go all over the known world to reveal the Father's heavenly agenda. Here is where He discovers Peter and

Andrew, who were in the vocation of fishing.

I really don't know how long they had been doing this, but by the content of the gospel in Matthew, we find that they seem to be really into it. They had made a living out of it, I mean, they owned boats, so their vocation appears to be a serious one.

All of us who have come into the kingdom of God know exactly in what position or predicament we were in before we gave our hearts to God. We moved by the sound of our own intelligence. We did things as we saw them right. We established ideas that were handed-down to us by our parents, friends, and maybe even a bit of religion. We had some common sense, and so we applied it to the best of our ability.

What this got us was perhaps some education, a job, made us some friends, and maybe some enemies along the way. In man's eyes we had things going for us — in God's eyes we were displaced. Let me explain.

Displaced at Birth

When we are born, as we come out of our mother's womb, and we are immediately placed outside the "garden of Eden," if you will. God created Eden for us, but our sinful nature disqualifies us for such a blessed place. It is not until Jesus invites us to go through the Door, which happens to be Himself, that we discover the garden of Eden once again. Do you get me?

So for a great part of our lives, we are wandering around trying to make sense of it. Who are we? Who made us and why? Much confusion surrounds us as we are living displaced lives. It is not until we come into God's kingdom that we find our place in life, in God, and in destiny! As we pursue God, we discover in detail, our futures.

The Lord will take us from the place we are presently at, and He will place us at the place where He needs us to be. Yes, it is the place where we will bring the greatest glory to God, the place where true satisfaction can only be found.

We all have been to beautiful places in this great country of ours, but nothing is more beautiful than to experience the garden of Eden in our souls!

As Jesus is searching for men to follow Him, He sees two displaced fishermen. He basically tells them, "You have been fishing for fish, but follow me, and I will show you what a life placed in the center of God's will looks like!"

God is awesome!

3

The Making of An Idol

"But our God is in heaven;
He does whatever He pleases.
Their idols are silver and gold,
The work of men's hands.
They have mouths, but they do not speak;
Eyes they have, but they do not see;
They have ears, but they do not hear;
Noses they have, but they do not smell;
They have hands, but they do not handle;
Feet they have, but they do not walk;
Nor do they mutter through their throat.
Those who make them are like them;
So is everyone who trusts in them." (Psalm 115:3-8)

This morning while seeking the Lord's face, I came across this powerful passage in Psalm 115, and I'm telling you, the Lord spoke loud and clear regarding idolatry and how one creates their own idol.

Obviously, we know that the Hebrew children were surrounded by many Gentile nations and that those nations worshipped other gods. It was so natural for the Gentiles to build statues for themselves out of raw materials such as wood, gold, etc. They didn't know Jehovah God, so without thinking twice, they created their own idea of a god and worshipped it.

Now, the Hebrew children, had been strictly forewarned in their commandments to not worship or set any other gods before them. Apparently, this first commandment in Exodus 20, served its purpose and it seemed to be honored by all who followed Jehovah God. There existed a healthy fear of the Lord when it came to other idols, at least for a while.

In Psalm 115, the writer brings about this truth once again. He points out how those statues that Gentiles worshiped were really worthless. They don't speak, see, hear or smell; they can't touch, or walk, or much less speak. Then the Psalmist says, **"Those who make them are like them; so is everyone who trusts in them."** Hmm…

Here's what the Holy Spirit began to unveil to me:

He told me, David — makers of idols are people who don't have a revelation of who God is and what God desires. Makers of idols are people who tend to do with their own mind and heart, what they think they would like to happen in their own lives without the one true God being involved in it.

Makers of idols are people who create out of their empty heads, create with their own hands a reflection of the emptiness they have inside. You cannot create something you are not! You can't make something work that doesn't exist in your own being. You can only mirror what you have inside. It is truly inevitable!

Obviously, makers of idols in biblical times, made all kinds of idols, because that is the only thing that existed within them. They were empty in soul; the statues were empty in expression. Isn't that something?

In closing this meditation, remember, you can only create with your hands what you have in your soul. If the Spirit of God is absent in you, then you will not hear God. You will hear "self" (the fleshly part of you,) but not God (the spirit part of you). You will never be able to give consistently what you don't have!

4

The Spiritually-Minded Servant

"For the mind-set of the flesh is death, but the mind-set of the Spirit is life and peace." (Romans 8:6) *Holman Christian Standard Bible*

Being in the presence of some brothers this past week, I realized something about people's understanding of the deeper life in God. What a deeper life in God means to some is not the same thing that it means to others. As a matter of fact, I find that many people's insight into God is not spiritually discerned as it should, but rather misinterpreted to accommodate fleshly desires and the like.

Pondering deeper on this, I also realized that some are not looking for God's agenda in the sermons they hear but they are instead truly focusing on what the message or sermon can do for them!

The Spiritually-Minded Servant

I know that sometimes, a meditation of this sort can ruffle some feathers, or make me sound like a "a holier than thou" individual. It is not my intent to beat anybody up spiritually-speaking, but it is my heart's desire to teach and educate God's man or woman to understand the deeper spiritual life in God.

The life in the Spirit is a life that focuses on God's agenda. It captures the essence of true kingdom living and power. It is a life that propagates God's heart and mind on the earth. As the Scriptures say, **"Thy kingdom come, thy will be done on earth as it is in heaven."**

Living in the Spirit is a life that has downloaded God's mind and works toward manifesting it here on earth. Basically, a spiritually-minded man or woman lives for accomplishing God's kingdom on earth.

The Carnally-Minded Servant

The carnal minded individual is pretty much the opposite of the spiritually-minded man. They focus on their own agenda, their own ideas, and look to be known by man not by God. The carnal-minded man is one who processes life through self! It's all about them, their name, their service, their reputation, their status, their plans.

When studying the word of God, they are really looking for intellectual information. They feel that the more they know, the more they are above others. The carnally-minded servant is a smart, sharp, intellectual person— but an unbroken person.

Brokenness as a Requirement

Until a person reaches the place of death, and their spirit is baptized into Christ, then and only then, can this person be led by the Spirit of God. The Spirit of God will find a home in a surrendered, broken and unselfish person! Once this happens, the person can now enjoy the riches of heaven and apply them powerfully into their life.

Let me close this meditation by saying that once a person has decided to enter into God by yielding themselves fully to Him, the Spirit of God will come and show that being the whole truth about kingdom living.

5

We See in Part Only!

"For now we are looking in a mirror that gives only a dim (blurred) **reflection** [of reality as in a riddle or enigma], **but then** [when perfection comes] **we shall see in reality and face to face! Now I know in part** (imperfectly), **but then I shall know and understand fully and clearly, even in the same manner as I have been fully and clearly known and understood** [by God]." (1 Corinthians 13:12) *Amplified Bible*

Here is an interesting meditation I penned earlier this week.

When a servant of God allows themselves to be educated by the things that surrounds them, they must always keep in consideration that the things being taught are only "in part." People only get tidbits of what God is really trying to express.

Often times, we pray for things to materialize, because we believe that we should get this or that— so, when things don't appear as we think they should, we often lose heart. We will get discouraged and start doubting.

What we must always keep before us, is that God does things in part, not in their entirety! What a lesson to apprehend if we can truly allow ourselves to be educated in this way. Everything that we learn on a daily basis is only a part of something greater and more complete.

To allow ourselves into believing that what we have learned is the fullness of it, would be to set ourselves for great disappointment at best!

I have seen through my own eyes, how servants of the Lord get so excited about an answered prayer or a breakthrough in their lives. They express continuous joy for this UNTIL they discover that what they received was only a portion of what was to come!

The wise servant of the Lord knows that what he has received up to now, is only in part and thus, rejoices with the part, but with great expectation looks forward to a greater revelation of what is to come! This is the order!

Before I close my mediation, let me add also that when God reveals "a part," there has to be a humility in us to receive it. The small morsel of revelation knowledge received with gratitude — will pave the way for the second part, and those there after. Every part lays out a wider foundation for the next part to come and sit upon it! Brick upon brick until the complete picture appears.

6

The Touch of Grace!

"But by the grace of God I am what I am, and His grace toward me was not in vain; but I labored more abundantly than they all, yet not I, but the grace of God which was with me." (1 Corinthians 15:10)

"For who has known the mind of the Lord that he may instruct Him? But we have the mind of Christ." (1 Corinthians 2:16)

This early morning, I had a visitation from the Lord and He disclosed this wonderful truth to me that I long to share with you. The truth has to do with His touch of grace upon our lives.

I know that so often we don't really acknowledge some of the great things God is doing in us and through us, or as a good friend of mine says, "We don't count our blessings, and we need to!"

While I meditated upon the letter that the Apostle Paul gave the Corinthian church, I read the portion where Paul says, **"But by the grace of God I am what I am..."** What does this really mean?

Basically, what Paul was saying was that God didn't waste His grace upon him. It's almost as if Paul in essence, is saying, "When I received God's grace, it gave me the understanding of what to do with my life, and therefore I labored more abundantly."

My friend, if it had not been for God's grace, Paul would have continued on the path of destruction. You and I were on the path of destruction, but God's grace was immense and more than able to give us a hope and a future. We became recipients of this grace and now we get to experience all that God had intended for us.

Now let me say that His grace is revealed in that He gave us His mind.

To have the mind of Christ is to have the mind of God.

Once the mind of God is attained in us, we get to know all that we need to know about His life, our life, our future, and the steps to walk out our destiny with great victory and confidence.

To discover the riches of all that God has promised, becomes a passionate delight and to fulfill the Father's wishes becomes the order of every single day of our lives. What a life in the mind of God!

If we don't enter into His mind, then our lives are void of motion and reality. We live but not under His will; we move but not at the rhythm of heaven.

When God is in us and we are in Him, then every thought counts; every movement counts. Every desire counts, and every breath counts. His mind changes everything! It changed the life of Peter the fisherman; it changed the life of Saul of Tarsus; it changed us to become His expressions on the earth!

Without His mind, how would we think? Without His mind, how would we act? Without His mind, what would we pursue? Without His mind we would be slaves to our own carnal mind— and this leads only one way, to corruption!

Thanks be to God that He chose us from the foundations of the world to reveal His Son Jesus in us!

Remember: *The future belongs to those who are led by His grace and His mind!*

7

Those Who Fear Him!

"He does not delight in the strength of the horse;
He takes no pleasure in the legs of a man.
The Lord takes pleasure in those who fear Him,
In those who hope in His mercy." (Psalm 147:10)

One of the most amazing things I have come to learn by reaching out and becoming friends with sinners, is the mindset they practice, and how they put their trust in things that are erroneous.

If they knew what a man or woman who has been born-again knew, they would never even consider putting their trust in vain things! So, for the most part, the prayers of those who have not been born-again, are offered as prayers of mercy and sometimes they are answered. All along God is giving them an excuse to believe in Him!

Let us see what God really thinks and feels about humanity's methods of trust. For that we will meditate on the Scripture I provided above.

First of all, God doesn't delight or take pleasure "in the strength of the horse or in the legs of man." This is what armies in Biblical times used to put their trust on. They used to trust their cavalry their weapons, etc. The greater a nation's army was, the more trust and confidence they had in winning any battle. This thought alone would make a king or commander proud and self-confident. It was this attitude that would make God not delight in them!

Is it any wonder why people who think that they know what to do and how to do it, always end up losing or lacking?!

For a believer to put their trust in their own strength, wisdom, intellect or abilities, is to send God a message that says, "I know you are God, but I got this. Thanks God but no thanks!" To not acknowledge God with all that you have is to slap Him on the face with pride!

Now in the same Psalm, the Psalmist instructs what God is really into. The Scripture reads the following: **"The Lord takes pleasure in those who fear Him. In those who hope in His mercy!"**

Wouldn't you want to know what unlocks the windows of God's favor upon your life? Wouldn't you want to know how to win every battle and never ever lose again? Well, it's all here and it's free!

The Lord takes pleasure in those who "fear" Him. What does the word "fear" mean in this context? The word "fear" means to show reverence; to stand in awe.

What the Lord truly wants is for us to revere Him, to acknowledge Him as our all and all. Though we might be powerfully equipped with all the wisdom, knowledge, ability, and man power, God wants to see how we react in relation to Him— when we have all these things to help us.

Will we gloat in ourselves and our abilities, or will we humble ourselves in the sight of the Lord for every victory?!

8

The Life of God in You!

"We are hard-pressed on every side, yet not crushed; we are perplexed, but not in despair; persecuted, but not forsaken; struck down, but not destroyed—always carrying about in the body the dying of the Lord Jesus, that the life of Jesus also may be manifested in our body. For we who live are always delivered to death for Jesus' sake, that the life of Jesus also may be manifested in our mortal flesh. So then death is working in us, but life in you." (2 Corinthians 4:8-12)

Meditating during my quiet time this morning, I came across this one powerful passage where the Apostle Paul discloses some intimate details about what has been the fountain of life that he manifested throughout his ministry.

One would probably venture and say that Paul was special because he was a very intelligent man. After all, Paul had been trained by some of the best teachers in the land during his youth before his conversion to Christ.

As valuable as all the information was to Saul of Tarsus (now Apostle Paul), all his understanding needed to be passed through God's fire. Most of his learning was done under the name of religion and for the benefit of status, not God's glory.

Most of us have read the conversion of Saul on the road to Damascus (Acts 9) and what a glorious encounter that was for this man. He was literally touched by God and called to suffer for Christ's sake.

During Paul's journeys, he experienced much adversity. As we would say, "He went through the mill!" All his experiences did not make him bitter, but better! He rose to become one of the most powerful voices in the earth for Jesus sake!

The Distinguishing Factor

The distinguishing factor in Paul's life was the brokenness that he went through to have God's message made real in him. It was definitely not a time of information anymore but a time of revelation— a revelation of who Jesus was and what Christ was all about. It was time to learn Christ— not of Christ! Christ was now the subject and the Holy Spirit would be the teacher.

Paul understood that from the day of his conversion, things would be very different. Every experience would be a mirror of the sufferings of Christ. The betrayals, the criticisms, the shaming, the dishonors, etc.... all of it, was meant to take him deeper in the life of God.

Here's Paul's philosophy of suffering for Jesus sake: **"For we who live are always delivered to death for Jesus' sake, that the life of Jesus also may be manifested in our mortal flesh. So then death is working in us, but life in you."**

Paul knew that daily there was a death sentence following him. The more Paul died to self, the more the life of God would be injected into him, if you can picture that? The more that he was rejected, the more he was embraced by God. He knew and understood that to suffer was truly the highway to the life of God in him.

The ministry of life that flowed from Paul was exactly what people would touch and feel when they got around him. People experienced God in the most real of ways, when they came in contact with this man of God, and Paul understood that unless there would be breaking— there would be no life of God flowing from him!

9

Who Is Calling the Shots?
Your Flesh or His Spirit?

"...while we do not look at the things which are seen, but at the things which are not seen. For the things which are seen are temporary, but the things which are not seen are eternal." (2 Corinthians 4:18)

This week I have been pondering the way we confront our circumstances, adversities and pressures in life. Though we all have our own battles to confront, and though we all have to face the floods of adversity (mind you, sometimes they come in bunches), we are responsible for the response we give to our adversity.

Our outcome will always depend upon our understanding of the world we live in. When I say "world," I am speaking of the spiritual condition we tend to pursue, set our affection upon, and/or let it influence us on a daily basis. Our "world" can be a carnal mindset or a spiritual one.

If your heart is set on the affliction that you are presently facing— you might end up very discouraged by it. The reason being is that the affliction that you are seeing is triggered by laws that govern it. Afflictions tend to hold people in boxes— thought boxes. When you see a giant coming towards you, the common response is to flee the danger or ignore it, but hardly ever to challenge it!

To try to fix, challenge, or change an affliction with the same laws that govern it— would be a recipe for disaster! One must see exactly the root cause of that affliction, and then challenge it with God's wisdom. You don't fight flesh with flesh...you will never win that battle!

The Scripture above says, **"we do not look at the things which are seen, but at the things which are not seen."**

When looking at a challenge, we should never see it for

what it is. Never succumb to it until you learn from what hand it is coming from. Either God or the flesh are pushing it. Either God or the flesh are pushing it. If the Lord, we embrace His discipline— if the flesh, we resist it!

We don't succumb to its laws, order, threats, or fears. We look at what is not seen, that is to say, we look at the spiritual realm for strategy. We trust God for the answer to come.

When we allow ourselves to ascend into God's dimension, the spiritual realm, then we will better understand what is at stake. We will see clearly who the culprit is, and how to overthrow it!

Next time you encounter affliction in your life, don't panic! Don't look at what your natural eyes are seeing— that is not a true picture of God's order and plan for your life. Ask the Lord to open your eyes and see the real issue, the real picture of what is fighting you, ensnaring you, discouraging you or overpowering you!

Only then, can you get a true understanding and receive specific strategy from heaven to overcome in Jesus' Name.

Paul knew that daily there was a death sentence following him. The more Paul died to self, the more the life of God would be injected into him, if you can picture that? The more that he was rejected, the more he was embraced by God. He knew and understood that to suffer was truly the highway to the life of God in him.

The ministry of life that flowed from Paul was exactly what people would touch and feel when they got around him. People experienced God in the most real of ways, when they came in contact with this man of God, and Paul understood that unless there would be breaking— there would be no life of God flowing from him!

10

Is Your Vessel Ready for God's Crucial Hour?!

"Then He came to the disciples and found them sleeping, and said to Peter, 'What! Could you not watch with Me one hour? Watch and pray, lest you enter into temptation. The spirit indeed is willing, but the flesh is weak.'" (Matthew 26:40-41)

Today's meditation comes from a simple lesson the Spirit taught me this past week regarding our willingness to be used by the Spirit of the Lord.

One would think that following God is such a noble thing to do and that it should be in everyone's priority list, and if possible, at the very top of that list.

People talk about following and obeying the Holy Spirit wherever He goes, etc.
After following Jesus for at least a good thirty-years of my

adult life, I have come to understand a few things in manners pertaining to obedience and willingness to follow Christ.

The story mentioned above is the one I want to revisit with you. It's the story of Jesus at Gethsemane. Here is Jesus in perhaps one of His darkest moments and in the greatest need for some type of support as He cried vehemently to the Father!

Jesus had only one request of His disciples, listen to this: **"Then Jesus came with them to a place called Gethsemane, and said to the disciples, 'Sit here while I go and pray over there.'** (Matthew 26:36)

His request was simple, **"Sit here while I go and pray over there."** Was this too much to ask? Was He really dropping a heavy demand upon them? Was He pushing too hard for them to stand with Him in this need of prayer?

Apparently, the disciples were tired and consequently fell asleep! When Jesus came back to see how they were doing,

He found them sleeping! He blasted them for not staying awake at the most crucial of moments saying, "What? Could you not watch with Me one hour?" He proceeds to warn them regarding temptation overtaking them for the lack of prayer and says, **"The Spirit indeed is willing, but the flesh is weak."**

Let me now turn your attention to this awesome revelation. See, the Spirit is indeed willing to do all that God desires to do. It is the Spirit's nature to flow with God's divine order. The Spirit of God is the mind of God and so it finds the need to move at the Father's heartbeat— the Father's request.

Only One Problem!

To all the moves of God, there seems to always be an opposition. The opposition is not really what you are thinking. As a matter of fact, the opposition is hardly ever what believer's think it is. The opposition that I'm referring to is the one Jesus pointed out— the flesh is weak!

God's desire is to release His dreams, visions, plans, and holy ambitions to you for the purpose of kingdom expansion. Only problem is, your support system, your body and mind are not available for increase. The Spirit indeed is willing; but your flesh is not!

Now the word "willing" in the Greek means to be "ready," "willing," "eager," even "active," or "passionate." So, the Spirit of the Lord is always ready to run, but our flesh is usually nowhere near the state of mind of the Spirit of God! Is this your case?

Flesh Must Be Brought Under Subjection!

The reason the flesh is not willing is because it is not subject to the Spirit of God who lives within you.

When God calls, our flesh is the first one to respond and say, "Sorry God, I'm not available for service at this moment! Call back later!"

Or "Sorry Lord, I'm don't feel up to par, or I'm not in the mood today. I'm a bit scared, I'm a bit doubtful, or I'm a little under the weather, consequently God, I won't be joining You in doing Your will. Check back later and I'll let you know how I feel by then."

God is always willing! The flesh must be dealt with and brought under God's divine order for it to be your servant. If we don't bring our flesh under subjection, we will never go anywhere with the Lord!

11

Learning to Grow!

**"Better is a little with the fear of the Lord,
Than great treasure with trouble."** (Proverbs 15:16)

"Be Patient!" These are probably two of the most hated words to the human ear. No one wants to be a participant of the growth process. In other words, we all want to grow, but if we could, we would like to "modify" the growth process!

Let me share with you this meditation that I have been chewing on for a while.

Let us first look at the Scripture mentioned above: **"Better is a little with the fear of the Lord..."** What does this mean? When one walks in the fear of the Lord, it means that there is God's structure in your life. This includes order and boundaries laid out for your life-not to hinder you, but rather to protect you from thinking that you are something when you are not! The fear of the Lord will keep us in our rightful place and deliver us from pride and arrogance.

The fear of the Lord is perhaps one of the best pace-makers for the human tendency of trying to be someone you are not ready to become yet!

What is Fleshly Increase?

Too often people can't discern the difference between what God gives and what is self-attained with selfish ambition. We tend to look at any type of increase as coming from the Lord when there has been no trajectory or history of being intimate with Christ.

To put it plainly, unless a person is intimate with Christ, there can be no heavenly deposit or seed. Either your flesh is impregnating you or the Spirit of God! Let this sink into your spirit.

Many will be content when they see the "great treasure" and little do they know of the trouble attached to it!

It is not until they start boasting of all that they have acquired, that the headaches begin. Anybody can say that God blessed them with this or that, but was it God? As my pastor used to always say to me, "David, anybody can convince themselves that they bought a good used car!"

The Art of Growing

When a man begins to grow God's way, it will be through the leadership of the fear of the Lord. The appreciation for every single step taken, every inch upward, every prompting of God's Spirit, will be immense.

Lastly, the temptation to be someone you are not ready to become and understanding this— will be key to the growth process. To know and/or recognize when it's time to take steps forward is truly an art. Many failed at this juncture in their spiritual life. The fear of the Lord will be your guide as you grow in God.

12

The House of Your Dreams!

"Prepare your outside work,
Make it fit for yourself in the field;
And afterward build your house." (Proverbs 24:27)

When an individual sets his heart to know and under-stand wisdom— a good place to start this endeavor would be in the book of Proverbs. The words of King Solomon in Proverbs are very practical and coupled with the fear of the Lord, any servant that wants to know the will of God, will find it!

The principle laid out in the verse above, or at least what the Holy Spirit has been showing me, is that God IS a God of order and does all His work based on His nature, not our own human nature.

"Prepare your outside work, make it fit for yourself in the field..." the Scripture starts of saying. Any builder understands that unless a good foundation has been laid out— the durability of a structure placed on top of it, might not be stable enough for floods or strong winds.

In dealing with any type of edifice, whether it is building yourself a good life, a good marriage, a good ministry or business— the wise would attend to the "outside work" first. Does everybody think like this? Of course not. This explains the constant collapse of the things mentioned.

The "outside work" of Proverbs 24 speaks to us about a solid foundation that will last for years and years to come. Building a foundation can never be taken lightly or nonchalantly.

In building a foundation, one must dig and dig till they find the bedrock before they can start building up. Who would dare build their foundation on mud? No one would think of doing such a thing and yet because of the time it takes to build a solid foundation, many choose the easy road and take the shortest route. This gives reason for most downfalls and early terminations.

Now providing that you have built a good foundation, you are now ready to build the house of your dreams, as the Scripture reads, **"and afterward build your house."**

Building a foundation is the equivalency of finding favor with God in all things. Teaching yourself to observe all that God desires for you is definitely a good foundational key for all your future developments.

The temptation for all of us will always be to hurry-up the process of building the foundation, so we can really get on with what is pretty and tangible; I'm speaking of walls, doors, windows, and furniture, etc.

No one looks or even cares for the foundations laid out. Rarely will anyone say, "Wow! Did you take a look at that cement foundation?! I wonder how deep it goes underground?"

Any project built upon Christ the solid Rock is a guaranteed-expression of His divine nature and love. Though it takes long to build it— it will be worth it!

As I close this meditation, keep in mind this key: First the outside (foundation) then the outside house. This is divine order!

13

Why I Am Not Quitting on Jesus!

"Therefore many of His disciples, when they heard this, said, 'This is a hard saying; who can understand it?' When Jesus knew in Himself that His disciples complained about this, He said to them, 'Does this offend you? What then if you should see the Son of Man ascend where He was before? It is the Spirit who gives life; the flesh profits nothing. The words that I speak to you are spirit, and they are life. But there are some of you who do not believe.' For Jesus knew from the beginning who they were who did not believe, and who would betray Him. And He said, 'Therefore I have said to you that no one can come to Me unless it has been granted to him by My Father.'

From that time many of His disciples went back and walked with Him no more. Then Jesus said to the twelve, 'Do you also want to go away?' But Simon Peter answered Him, 'Lord, to whom shall we go? You have the words of eternal life. Also we have come to believe and know that You are the Christ, the Son of the living God.'" (John 6:60-69)

When was the last time you had a challenge so big in your life that you actually thought you weren't going to make it? When was the last time you felt so overwhelmed with despair and failure that you said to yourself, "I will not survive the storm this time around!"

In your fear, in your despair, in your discouragement, in the middle of it all, there seemed to appear a little ray of hope— a still small voice that said, "I got you! I'm not letting go of your hand. Just keep holding on through this season, this dry patch, this unexplainable test!"

Too often in our despair we tend to get shaken by the things that surround us. In can happen to anyone and at any time. By the time you know it, the flood of testing will visit you and attempt to bring you to a place of no return.

I'm not sure what all the conversation was between Jesus and His disciples, but it appeared to me that some just had a hard time coming to grips with the expectations of Jesus. Some might have been offended at His words, others might just not have been up to speed with what Christ was saying to them. All I know is that Jesus was speaking in spiritual terms and some of the followers didn't get it!

After His discourse, many followers of Jesus decided to turn back. I'm sure it wasn't easy for them to quit on Christ; yet, they didn't or couldn't understand the vision of Jesus, therefore, they had no sustaining power to keep them following.

Do You Want To Leave Also?

After seeing the masses walk away from Him, Jesus looked at His faithful twelve disciples and said to them, "Are you guys quitting too?"

When all hell breaks loose on you, and when all you ever believed, is put through the fire, when all you have ever banked on seems to be shaking – then Christ comes to us and says, "Are you leaving too?"

Listen to Peter's words: **"Lord, to whom shall we go? You have the words of eternal life. Also we have come to believe and know that You are the Christ, the Son of the living God."** Is there anything more powerful to sustain a man or a woman of God than to acknowledge the fact, **"Lord, to whom shall we go? You have the words of eternal life."**

Time after time, I have come to this place in my own life... where there is nothing to hold on to and no one to hold on to, but the basic fact of His words is all I got: "Where am I really going to go? No one knows me like Jesus, no one cares for me like Jesus, and no one understands me like Jesus! I'm going to hold onto the hem of His garment until the breakthrough and/or the blessing comes!"

14

Chill Out! God Is Only Working in You.

"The end of a thing is better than its beginning;
The patient in spirit is better than the proud in spirit.
Do not hasten in your spirit to be angry,
For anger rests in the bosom of fools.
Do not say, 'Why were the former days better than these?'
For you do not inquire wisely concerning this."

(Ecclesiastes 7:8-10)

In pondering these few verses during my quiet time, I came across this tremendous revelation of how God works in us and moves us from glory to glory.

You know very well, that God is a progressive God; He brought us out (from a life of sin and corruption) to bring us into a life of abundance and blessing! As we grow in the revelation of Him, He gives accordingly. To the degree we increase in our foundation, is to the degree of revelation, wisdom, and understanding He gives.

The End Is Better

The Scripture says that the end is better than its beginning. Why is this statement so powerful to those seeking increase in God or spiritual maturity?

When you have something in your heart that you want to do, the beginning is really the easiest part to it. Anyone with any amount of will-power can set themselves on a course that seems promising. The human mind is a gift from God, and one can use it to glorify God or glorify themselves.

Anyone can convince themselves that the course they are on is truly the right one and pursue with determination and commitment until it is achieved.

Here is why "the end is better."

What happens in you, is way better than you getting to your desired end. What God will do in your inner-man is way more powerful than your answered prayer. The Scripture above goes on to say, **"The patient in spirit is better than the proud in spirit. Do not hasten in your spirit to be angry. For anger rests in the heart of fools."**

What this portion means is that once you have set yourself on a course, expect your heart and mind to be worked on by the Holy Spirit. Your impatient heart and mind will be shattered until you become gentle, pliable, and submissive to God's order.

The Former Days Are Not Better!

The temptation is always to go back into the past and try to relive it. To enter into a state of nostalgia and reminisce about all the great things of yesterday. Many people are trapped in this state of thinking. Don't let that be you! Be a person of revelation and progressiveness in God!

Listen to the Scripture: Do not say, "Why were the former

days better than these? For you do not inquire wisely concerning this."

So often we don't see where God is taking us. We only see and focus on the last good moment we experienced, and then become totally unaware of the new lands and/or opportunities God has prompted us to conquer!

The Scripture teaches us to "Not say, 'Why were the former days better than these?'" The real reason for this exhortation is very simple: Yesterday is not better than the now!

You see, today, we have entered into new ground. We have new giants to conquer; this will teach us to trust God in a greater way. It will teach us to increase in faith, to grow in our new-found confidence in God. It teaches us to develop a listening spiritual ear— so we may receive instruction to progress in the new chapter God is mercifully unfolding before us. If we can see it, we can possess it!

As I close this meditation, please chill out! Don't concern

yourself with matters that are irrelevant to your increase. While learning the art of allowing God to have His way, set your affection on things above, not on things of the earth! Stay hidden in Christ as you learn His ways!

15

The Delicateness of Intimacy with God! - Part 1

"I sleep, but my heart is awake;
It is the voice of my beloved!
He knocks, saying,
'Open for me, my sister, my love,
My dove, my perfect one;
For my head is covered with dew,
My locks with the drops of the night.'
I have taken off my robe;
How can I put it on again?
I have washed my feet;
How can I defile them?
My beloved put his hand
By the latch of the door,
And my heart yearned for him.
I arose to open for my beloved,
And my hands dripped with myrrh,

My fingers with liquid myrrh,
On the handles of the lock.
I opened for my beloved,
But my beloved had turned away and was gone.
My heart leaped up when he spoke.
I sought him, but I could not find him;
I called him, but he gave me no answer." (Song of Solomon 5:2-6)

In meditating upon the subject of intimacy with God this past week, I came across this subject matter in Song of Solomon chapter 5. As I read this particular portion I came to the realization of how fine and delicate is this intimacy with God.

Now the word intimacy in the dictionary is defined as— a close, familiar, and usually affectionate or loving personal relationship with another person or group.

So then by definition, we know that intimacy has to do with affection. Without affection, one would have such a hard time developing any type of relationship with anyone or even coming to the place of sharing inward desires and secrets of the heart.

The Father longs to be intimate with us His children. It is the desire of God that we love Him and experience the reciprocation of His love for us as well

.

An Awakened Heart!

"I sleep, but my heart is awake; It is the voice of my beloved!" Anytime that I come across this verse, my heart leaps within me because of this one scenario.

The scenario of someone sleeping but awake in the inward parts. When our hearts are awake during the day or night, (as if standing guard) waiting for something awesome to take place;this is what I picture here.

The writer says, **"It is the voice of my beloved!"** What this means is that through the night, in restlessness of spirit, this individual's heart has been longing or yearning for this moment, the beloved's voice!

Intimacy with God always has its initial beginnings introduced by a restlessness of spirit. The characteristic that I see consistently in those who seek intimacy with God is the one where they are unsettled as if something was missing from them. Yet all the while, an invitation to be intimate with God is about to be downloaded into that hungry heart.

The Request

Then, the invitation arrives. Listen to this:

"He knocks, saying,
'Open for me, my sister, my love,
My dove, my perfect one;
For my head is covered with dew,
My locks with the drops of the night.'
I have taken off my robe;

**How can I put it on again?
I have washed my feet;
How can I defile them?"**

The invitation comes first by form of request. First, the Lord will request that we open the door for Him, so He may come in and be intimate with us. Let me tell you that these are the best encounters any human being can experience this side of God's literal glory.

Unless the Lord is invited first to come in and reveal His heart to us, we will not have the ability to see God's pattern for our lives.

Remember, it takes God to know God.

16

The Delicateness of Intimacy with God! - Part 2

"My beloved put his hand
By the latch of the door,
And my heart yearned for him.
I arose to open for my beloved,
And my hands dripped with myrrh,
My fingers with liquid myrrh,
On the handles of the lock." (Song of Solomon 5:4-5)

In my study of the Delicateness of Intimacy with God, I have discovered that unless one lends his time and full attention to a subject, one can really learn that subject or not. One can excel in knowing and understanding something valuable or not. It is all dependent upon how much determination we have to stay focused on something of value.

Is it hard for God to get a hold of you?

In my last meditation, I covered the subject of how God comes to us and requests that we open the door for Him to come in and be intimate with us.

Today, it is my desire to bring you into something a little deeper: What it means to be conscious of God's persuasion of you. How God not only requests that we allow Him to come in, but that we are fully conscious of His desire to meet us and be with us in the most intimate of ways!

Too often we are present in body but not in mind and heart!

In the Scripture above, I find that God (the Beloved) is putting His hand by the latch of the door.

Don't Make It Hard for God to Find You!

Here is one thing I know about God…He knows us! He knows us so well that we can't hide anything from Him. He knows and understands our frailties; He sees our fears and doubts!

When Adam and Eve had sinned against God back in Genesis 3, man hid from God. Hiding from the Lord is a typical response of guilt and shame before Him. He knows we have sinned — so it does us no good to hide. I'm sure you already know this, but let me remind you, He already knows, and by us "shutting down" God, it is not going to make it any better. Why? Because He loves us and doesn't want us to be separated from Him. He will track us down and find us.

I believe the Lord comes to us just like in this verse. His hand opens up the latch and we know it is Him! The way we know this is simple — our heart is filled with a yearning for Him. The word yearning here in the Hebrew means, "to growl" to be disturbed."

Every time God is near, our hearts begin to burn with excitement and everything in us leaps!

Can you imagine the thought of having Jesus coming to

your house for dinner? What a revolution in your inner-most being! You would become stirred! You would head out to your local expensive furniture store and purchase a nice dining table and chair set, prepare an extravagant meal, polish and paint your house, do your landscape all over again. I bet a serious investment would be made, why? Because the King is coming to visit you! Your heart would be growling with excitement.

There is no need to hide from Jesus. He is all loving and all caring and desires intimacy with us. He longs for us to be aligned with His plan. Remember: His blood washes our sins and restores us to His favor. Be sensitive to His visitations. He desires to be intimate with us.

17

The Delicateness of Intimacy with God! - Part 3

"I opened for my beloved,
But my beloved had turned away and was gone.
My heart leaped up when he spoke.
I sought him, but I could not find him;
I called him, but he gave me no answer." (Song of Solomon 5:6)

In meditating upon the subject of intimacy, I have also come to the realization that I have a rebellious stubborn heart that fights for its "rights." The "rights" to rule and do my own thing!

In God, and for those who walk with Him, we know all too well that God desires for us to follow His lead, His ways.

We can follow God by being told by His Spirit what to do, or we can follow God by discerning His wishes. In other words, this means doing His will without being told what to do and when. This is definitely a more mature approach to pursuing the heart of God.

Why Are We Too Slow to Respond?

As I read this portion in Song of Solomon 5:6, I saw something that caught my attention. After that the Beloved (God) had been trying to open the latch of the door, it seems to be that the door was never opened.

All kinds of questions fill my heart at this point.

For one: Why was not the door opened fast enough? I mean after all, it was the Beloved wanting to come in and have intimacy with His bride.

Was the latch stuck? Was it broken? Did it have a lock that we don't know of? I don't know. All I know is that the door was never opened for intimacy.

Are there things in our lives that are keeping our hearts under lock and key? Are we "shying" away from God's heart? Are we not feeling His need for intimacy with us? Why are we not having intimacy with God?

Where Did the Beloved Go?

The Scripture goes on to say that by the time the bride got up to open the door, the Beloved had taken off! He had turned away and was gone! She spoke to him, but He gave her no answer ...is this tragic or what?

My dear friends, if there is something we need to get accustomed to is this: God wants to be intimate with us! He longs to meet us and be with us all the time. It is His nature to be intimate with us.

The next time the Lord comes knocking at the door of our hearts, we must be quick to recognize it. We must be quick to hear and obey His wishes!

18

Putting Away Your Idol!

**"You shall have no other gods before Me.
You shall not make for yourself a carved image—any likeness of anything that is in heaven above, or that is in the earth beneath, or that is in the water under the earth; you shall not bow down to them nor serve them. For I, the Lord your God, am a jealous God..."** (Exodus 20:3-5)

Pondering on God's intent when Moses penned this verse, is both sobering and very convicting.

Nothing moved the heart of God more with anger and jealousy than when His people would follow hand-made idols. It was in His heart that His people would only love, worship and serve Him only! To do anything other than what God was wishing for, would be very disappointing to God.

On the list of His commandments, Jehovah God made it very plain and clear in the book of Exodus. He outlined it and had Moses teach it as one of God's divine order principles.

What Is Idolatry, Really?

Well, for starters, idolatry is the worship of idols. Oxford Dictionary states that the word idolatry means extreme admiration, love, or reverence for something or someone. What is interesting to me is that God knew that there would be competition from other entities making every attempt to draw us away after them.

God knew that there would arise from within us an extreme admiration, love and reverence for something or someone else. He saw it coming and therefore warned us of this potential danger.

It Starts in the Heart!

One can have a profound love for things (books, shoes, purses, cars, jobs, etc and still remain pure to the allegiance of Christ. It's when the thing you love begins to love you back— that idolatry begins to take shape and the ensnaring begins.

Is it any wonder why God says, **"You shall not make for yourselves any carved images?"** The reason for His early warning is for us to dismantle the thought of having any love-relationship with anything other than Him!

God knew that once our hearts got a glimpse of something other than Him, we would be so easily persuaded to give ourselves to it. We would give our time, emotions, money, and in even in extreme circumstances, a great sacrifice!

God said, **"I am a jealous God!"** He wasn't going to have any of this plague His people be robbed of His glory in any way shape or form.

We can love a thing, but when God says, "Leave that

thing!" — we must be ready to drop it immediately. We must then be obedient— trust Him and follow Him!

19

Let This Mind Be In You!

"Let this mind be in you which was also in Christ Jesus, who, being in the form of God, did not consider it robbery to be equal with God, but made Himself of no reputation, taking the form of a bondservant, and coming in the likeness of men. And being found in appearance as a man, He humbled Himself and became obedient to the point of death, even the death of the cross. Therefore God also has highly exalted Him and given Him the name which is above every name, that at the name of Jesus every knee should bow, of those in heaven, and of those on earth, and of those under the earth, and that every tongue should confess that Jesus Christ is Lord, to the glory of God the Father." (Philippians 2:5-11)

Our life in Christ is not just another life. Our life in Christ is not just another alternate way of living or getting by in life. Our life in Christ is not a set of religious ideas that turn us into religious extremist or freaks! No sir.

Our life in Christ is the pattern laid out by our heavenly Father— a heavenly divine order that mirrors God's heart, mind, and actions in the earthly regions.

In his letter to the Philippians, Paul brings forth such a beautiful picture of what a man IN Christ should be. The man who is IN Christ must have the mind of Christ, which is the mind of God. Let's break it down:

1. "Let this mind be in you which was also in Christ Jesus, who, being in the form of God, did not consider it robbery to be equal with God..."

The Apostle Paul brings us to the revelation of what Jesus was literally thinking as He made His way through the streets and shores of Galilee. He knew He was the Son of God and understood His equality with the Father. As you and I walk with God, we have this treasure within our lives that is so awesome; it is so wonderful that when we discover it, we become exuberantly emotional. God lives in us! What a wonder that is. Though we have the Creator of the universe living inside of us, we don't gloat, show off, or put others down because of their blindness. This is exactly what Jesus did— He did not gloat! He knew His place in the Father's plan.

2. ".. but made Himself of no reputation, taking the form of a bondservant, and coming in the likeness of men."

Instead of becoming a showoff, Jesus took a different road—the road of willfully making Himself of no reputation. He chose to put His title as Son of God away; He then took the form of a servant or slave. This way, Jesus could relate with the likeness of men. What an amazing move Jesus made when He became a bondservant! I mean, who does this? In the world we live today, most people want recognition and seek positions in the highest of places. Not Jesus!

3. "And being found in appearance as a man, He

humbled Himself and became obedient to the point of
death, even the death of the cross."

Because Christ Himself took the form of a man and a
bondservant at that, He was able to humble Himself to the
lowest point. He went as far as becoming obedient to the
point of death on a cross. Do you see this pattern of humility? Can you see how humility is the one characteristic
that outshines all the others in the life of Jesus Our Lord?
If a man cannot humble himself and forsake his own life,
there is just no way that that man can make a lasting im-
pact.

**4. "Therefore God also has highly exalted Him
and given Him the name which is above every name..."**

The benefits of a surrendered and humbled life are truly
powerful in God. You see, when one humbles himself and
takes the form of attitude that Christ lived out, God will
honor that person. It will be the Lord Himself exalting
you in the presence of your enemies. God will honor you

and prop you up to the highest places. This is the fruit of a servant who has put on the mind of Christ.

20

The Garden of Your Life

**"Awake, O north wind,
And come, O south!
Blow upon my garden,
That its spices may flow out."** (Song of Solomon 4:16)

While visiting my mother's grave a few days back, I came upon several cemetery plots. I must admit that some plots were very well kept: beautiful big oak trees and small trees covered in leafy foliage and the ground was decorated by a beautiful array of flowers.

It was obvious to me that many people do invest in cemetery plots and go all out to make sure that their loved ones are honored properly.

I have learned some things over the years, and one of the

things that I have come to learn and appreciate most— is the way a life of neglect can hurt us in more ways than one.

Initially, one might think that leaving something undone or pretending a problem is not really as big as people make it out to be, can be a telltale sign of an imminent problem.

In processing this meditation, the garden I want to speak of has to do with a neutral playing field. Whatever you plant, cultivate, and protect is what you will have as a testimony to the fruits of your labor.

One can either plant fruit or one can plant vegetables, and whatever is planted, must be attended to or else...or else nature will claim what belongs to it!

If one doesn't attend to his or her garden, they will end up having a field full of thorns and thistles. It will not be beautiful, and definitely much less fragrant. It will be a field that screams, Neglected!

If people would spend at least half the time they spend in fixing their gardens in fixing their lives— they would be victorious, fruitful, and joyful!

In planting the beautiful garden of our lives, one must then choose carefully what to sow or plant in it. You must be careful to plant things that are of value. Things that are important would be a good choice. The returns you get from planting something great in the garden of your life will be awesome!

After planting, one must then give themselves over to cultivating that precious garden. Cultivate means to develop. It is my belief that every human being should develop their own lives in the sight of the Lord. It is our responsibility to learn and grow as much as is within us. To acquire the skills and abilities to become such a magnificent tool in the hands of God should be our goal.

Lastly, one must protect what he or she believes is worth protecting. Too often we don't protect what is ours. If God gave us a life, then it has to be a good life! A life with vision and endless possibilities should be a motivating force for all who believe.

Don't let life pass you by! Don't let others take away from your garden! Don't let others put anything that would poison the flowers that produce the fragrance in your garden.

If there is anything that we owe man — is to grow our gardens as beautiful as we know how. Then we invite the wind of God to blow through it — so others may be amazed with such a fragrance, the fragrance of Jesus in us!

21

Until His Mercy Comes!

"Behold, as the eyes of servants look unto the hand of their masters, and as the eyes of a maiden unto the hand of her mistress; so our eyes wait upon the LORD our God, until that he have mercy upon us." (Psalm 123:2)

Here is an interesting take on the subject of waiting.

Too often, we believers, despair when it comes to being patient with situations in our daily life. We tend to get truly desperate when things are hard and it seems as though the flood waters are rising.

I believe that it is at this point, when our faith is truly tested, and our commitment to hold on to the promises of God, becomes a real challenge.

In my service unto the Lord, I have across many individuals who have been put through the ringer. Many have experienced extreme adversity and wonder how long will this testing endure.

The question always arises as to what one should do about this or that— or how does one know when to go or when to stop. There are many challenges in life, and if one doesn't know the Lord, one cannot find a way out of their own dilemma. It's almost impossible!

Not My Will But Yours Lord!

In studying the subject in more detail, I discovered as I read Psalm 123:2, that the servants set their eyes on the hands of their masters, not on their clocks or calendars! This accounts for something. I believe that there is something very deep there.

You see, the hand is where the provisions comes through. The servant is not looking at their need, but rather looking at when the master will release the blessing.

I believe God desires for us to gain a new whole concept about what it means to wait for direction, for advancement, etc. It is not until the master opens his hand, that the timing is right. If the master doesn't open his hand, then it is not time to receive! Do you see this?

To make demands of a master would be so out of order. It doesn't matter the need or how desperate you find yourself— no sir, it's about allowing the Lord to have His way in us until He sees fit to release exactly what we need. To go ahead of the master would be disrespectful and selfish.

We usually don't find out how selfish and self-deserving we truly are, until the fire is lit, and we enter the crucible of God—then we get to see ourselves as we really are!

As I close this word, I want to turn your attention to this one part of the Scripture: "So our eyes wait upon the LORD our God, until that he have mercy upon us."

The attitude of God's man is found on this one line: we (as

God's servants) will not dare make a move until God has mercy upon us! What does this really mean?

Until God has mercy means until God gives us the ok to proceed with the decision, the plan, or until God makes us feel peace regarding the decision taken or made. If God gives us peace, then we rest. If God doesn't give us peace, then we conclude that God still has yet to speak.

The goal of His mercy is so we can rest upon His approval, not our capricious attitude.

22

It Takes Wisdom to Touch a Life for Jesus!

"Walk in wisdom toward those who are outside, redeeming the time. Let your speech always be with grace, seasoned with salt, that you may know how you ought to answer each one." (Colossians 4:5-6)

As I meditated upon this one particular verse, I found some interesting insight into the heart of God as revealed by the Apostle Paul.

Paul's words to the Colossian church was that they were to "walk in wisdom toward those who are outside, redeeming the time." Who is outside? What time is Paul making reference to?

For starters, the Apostle Paul refers to those outside as to the lost, the sinner who is yet to come to Christ. He is bringing to the forefront, the idea that we believers, should always make it our aim to walk in wisdom, especially in the presence of those who are yet to be born into God's kingdom.

We are also to be conscious of the time we live in and be held responsible for where our time goes. As we live our lives, work at our place of work, etc. - we should be ever so conscious of time.

In using God's wisdom to touch the lost, Paul adds, **"Let your speech always be with grace, seasoned with salt, that you may know how you ought to answer each one."** There is nothing more attractive to a lost sinner, then a graceful person. When we exercise grace and our manner of speaking is intelligent and wise, the lost sinner will find himself captivated by such words and passion.

I read a survey that was given a few years ago, that stated the reasons of why lost sinners wanted nothing to do with the local church and its outreach. The lost sinner in this particular survey said that coming to church was not a good experience because of two key reasons. Listen to this:

1. Christians are too legalistic. They have to many laws, rules and rituals, which by the way, they don't even keep themselves.

2. Christians have a "holier than thou" attitude. Christians come across with the idea that puts them above everybody else, and they look down at the lost sinners as rejected citizens.

Obviously, this survey does make a lot of sense, if you have been in the Christian church for some time. It is true what these sinners are seeing! Christians are concerned about an idea and not about God's purpose for humanity.

Proverbs 11:30 reads: **"The fruit of the righteous is a tree of life, and he who is wise wins souls."** All this really means is that one must be wise if he or she is ever going to win a soul and bring them into the kingdom of God.

23

Don't Judge, there Is Still a Speck in Your Eye!

"Judge not, that you be not judged. For with what judgment you judge, you will be judged; and with the measure you use, it will be measured back to you. And why do you look at the speck in your brother's eye, but do not consider the plank in your own eye? Or how can you say to your brother, 'Let me remove the speck from your eye'; and look, a plank is in your own eye? Hypocrite! First remove the plank from your own eye, and then you will see clearly to remove the speck from your brother's eye." (Matthew 7:1-5)

What a tremendous piece of wisdom Jesus gave His followers! He literally balanced the playing field for all humanity. In short, Jesus made it known, that there is no one righteous — not a single one who is worthy to **"cast the first stone."** So, He continues His discourse and says, **"Judge**

not, that you be not judged."

Because you yourself are not who you think you are, one should not think higher than any other human being. When we look at life with understanding and with God's eyes and heart— we will learn what Jesus meant when He said, **"Those who are well have no need of a physician, but those who are sick. But go and learn what this means: I desire mercy and not sacrifice. For I did not come to call the righteous, but sinners, to repentance."** (Matthew 9:12, 13)

The compassion that Jesus practiced had to do with this understanding. It had to do with loving unconditionally even though one didn't deserve it. It was about reaching to the uttermost, even when it was not convenient to do so!

One might think that this is really a hard thing to do in the natural. It is! When we have been wronged, when we have been betrayed— all we think is how we can "get back" at that person or group, etc. We carry this spirit of revenge and all we want to do is see them pay back for all that they have done to us! We rejoice in their failures, we applaud (in secret of course) when something negative happens to them, etc. I know that you have been there— we all have!

In spite of all the wrong that has been caused, in spite of all the mistreatment we have received— we are called to not judge! We don't do it because we also have **"a speck in our eye!"** Our lives are not as perfect as we think they are. Just ask God!

To "judge" means to divide. To come to a conclusion. Jesus is telling us not to do it. Not to conclude a matter before the real Judge makes His final judgement. We are not called to be the judges of no man due to our inability to do it correctly. If we were perfect in every way, then maybe we could judge. But remember, not even Jesus did it. He would not even judge the woman caught in adultery.

Listen to the heart of God: **"Then the scribes and Pharisees brought to Him a woman caught in adultery. And** when they had set her in the midst, they said to Him, 'Teacher, this woman was caught in adultery, in the very act. Now Moses, in the law, commanded us that such should be stoned. But what do You say?' This they said, testing Him, that they might have something of which to accuse Him. But Jesus stooped down and wrote on the ground with His finger, as though He did not hear. So when they continued asking Him, He raised Himself up and said to them, 'He who is without sin among you, let him throw a stone at her first.' And again He stooped down and wrote on the ground. Then those who heard it, being convicted by their conscience, went out one by one, beginning with the oldest even to the last. And Jesus was left alone, and the woman standing in the midst. When Jesus had raised Himself up and saw no one but the woman, He said to her, 'Woman, where are those accusers of yours? Has no one condemned you?' She said, 'No one, Lord.' And Jesus said to her, 'Neither do I condemn you; go and sin no more.'" (John 8:3-11)

If anyone could have judged and condemned this woman, it would have been Jesus. If anyone had a right to throw a stone at this woman, it would have been Jesus; but He said, **"Neither do I condemn you!"**

24

What You and I Don't Know!

"No temptation has overtaken you except such as is common to man; but God is faithful, who will not allow you to be tempted beyond what you are able, but with the temptation will also make the way of escape, that you may be able to bear it." (1 Corinthians 10:13)

Temptation is a thing that happens to all who breathe on this planet. Temptation is not something reserved for special people, but rather for all the human race. How we deal with temptation is what produces spiritual authority in us.

We Don't Know!

As we navigate through this world empowered by the Holy Spirit, there are times, when for some odd reason, we come under such severe testing in our lives. Temptations of every sort begin to come upon us and we find ourselves at times, in despair and overwhelmed by it all.

Too often, people who face temptation, are usually pretty quiet about the battles they face. They don't want anyone to know about their shortcomings, their struggles and harsh battles with sin. So, they remain quiet.

When a dear brother or sister falls into sin or compromises their stand of holiness, there are several things that we who are on the outside fail to see in their demise:

1. For one, we don't know how hard they have been fighting this demon, this wicked temptation, this overwhelming urge that comes in like a flood upon them.

2. And secondly, we don't know how powerful this thing arrayed against them to bring them down, really is!

I know that it is easy to judge a brother or sister when he or she is down, but how many can be sensitive enough to raise them up and edify them when they are down and out? Our challenge is to stay close to the heart of Jesus and come in at the right time to help in time of need.

God Makes a Way Out!

In the Scripture above, we discover that temptation is common to all; we also find that God has provided a way of escape for all.

The secret to overcoming life is to be quick to hear the voice of God that says, "This is a trap against you...quick! —make your way to the escape door... run— don't walk!"

Nothing sustains a man more than a broken and contrite spirit. If one will humble himself before God, He will be able to stand against anything in any situation.

25

As It Is in Heaven!

"In this manner, therefore, pray:
Our Father in heaven,
Hallowed be Your name.
Your kingdom come.
Your will be done
On earth as it is in heaven." (Matthew 6:9-10)

In the Lord's prayer, Jesus alludes to something that not too many believers capture. It's not anything fancy or poetic, but it is tremendously rich in context. As a matter of fact, Jesus never prayed or said or did anything without celestial significance and/or consequence!

Jesus said, "In this manner, therefore, pray.." The Lord Himself was laying out a kingdom idea that would forever change the way true praying was to be conducted in private and in public.

The disciples of Jesus, in regard to prayer, said to Jesus, "teach us to pray." Jesus did!

The subject I want to bring before you, has more to do with the part that reads: "Your kingdom come. Your will be done, on earth as it is in heaven."

As Jesus lived His life on earth, He was not trying to show us how a human being should conduct himself or how a human being should speak or think. He was teaching everyone that our lives must be heavenly— directed and empowered. That the idea of how to live a life, and should be lived from the heavenly Father's perspective and not an earthly one.

Too often, people don't point us to the right source. They want us to live by man-made rules, which don't carry God's intent for humanity and the expansion of His kingdom.

Your Kingdom Come!

God's kingdom is the only right idea. There is not another idea that pleases the Father but this one! Our lives are perfectly defined from God's perspective. To get this perspective, one must ascend to the throne through prayer, and behold God's eternal pattern.

When you see the pattern that God has outlined for you to live out, then one can put all his strength and resources into following the idea that pleases the Father.

Your Will Be Done on Earth!

When one sees what exactly it is that God created us to be, and we start to understand that we must move according to this plan, His will— then we can begin making the necessary changes according to His pattern, not our pattern.

Yes, it is God's will that we must see and walk-out on a daily basis. It is the only thing that brings lasting change accompanied by an eternal consequence.

26

Earn the Degree in God!

"For those who have served well as deacons obtain for themselves a good standing and great boldness in the faith which is in Christ Jesus." (1 Timothy 3:13)

As I meditated upon these few words in the book of 1 Timothy 3, I came to this powerful portion of Scripture that gives out the secret of how one can be promoted in God.

In the letter to Timothy, Paul is giving Timothy much needed instruction on how to raise up good leadership to oversee the work of God. He is laying down some good foundational principles and makes it clear that if one can "pass the test," that one will be known and respected.

Let me turn your attention to the verse above: **"For those who have served well..."** What does it mean to serve

The Heart of David Journal

well? The word well means "to conceal; to bury." In other words, those who have served well, have done it in humility; they have served in Jesus' Name; they did it for the glory of God, not themselves. This is the first test for all servants of Jesus.

A second step to promotion would be — if they have served well, they would "obtain for themselves a good standing and great boldness in the faith..." The word standing means "a degree, a step."

If a servant of Jesus serves well in humility and contriteness of heart, this alone will put him in good standing; in other words, he will take a huge step forward or will earn a degree in the sight of God and man.

Anytime you and I are being tested in whatever area of our lives, we must have the eyes of God lest we disqualify ourselves from earning a degree in God. Every negative thing that will ever hit you here on earth is a set test for the earning of a degree. If one fails to see Jesus in all of the testing, one will not get that degree that will establish your leadership on earth.

Too often, many disqualify themselves from positions in the Lord, not because they are bad people, bad citizens, bad fathers or mothers; they disqualify themselves because they lack understanding of the inspection, they are under by the Holy Spirit.

God will allow His servants to give of themselves in service and then He will step back to see the attitude of what we show when we are criticized, praised, loved, trusted, and complimented, etc.

Our degree in God depends on how we handle every test we will ever face. Generations are waiting for our promotion in God.

27

Inside the Potter's Heart – Part 1

"The word which came to Jeremiah from the Lord, saying: 'Arise and go down to the potter's house, and there
I will cause you to hear My words.' Then I went down to
the potter's house, and there he was, making something
at the wheel. And the vessel that he made of clay was
marred in the hand of the potter; so he made it again into
another vessel, as it seemed good to the potter to make.
Then the word of the Lord came to me, saying: 'O house
of Israel, can I not do with you as this potter?'" (Jeremiah
18:1-6a)

Vessel in the Making

Of all the Scriptures in the Bible, here is one that has always profoundly intrigued me, being that it deals with the
making of a vessel that is presentable or useful. This has
always been God's heart — to complete the work He sets

in motion.

Jeremiah the prophet was being used by God during this era as a mouthpiece for the Lord. At this time in history, Judah had turned from following the Lord and given themselves to idol worship. God was not happy with any of it!

Jeremiah is now being sent by God to visit the potter's house with instructions to hear what God would tell him. Here's where we pick up our story...

As It Seemed Good to Him...

As the Prophet Jeremiah gets to the potter's house, the Lord opens the prophet's understanding.

First, Jeremiah sees the potter making something at the wheel. Why did he just see "something?" What was this "something?" For starters, the Hebrew definition of something means occupation; work. Jeremiah literally saw the Potter making or creating something that would be useful.

Jeremiah quickly understood the Potter's intent!

After this, Jeremiah noticed something else; he noticed, that the vessel of clay which the Potter was making was a bit unusual. The Scripture says that the vessel was marred. What does marred mean? The word marred means to go to ruin.

Jeremiah literally saw that the clay vessel was not good. It was ruined. So, the Potter made it again. The clay was then bathed with water again, and shaped one more time with the goal of making it perfect to the Potter's eye.

I really don't know how clay pottery works, but before the potter even begins their work, apparently, there is a finished product in the mind of the Potter. They begin their project with an end in mind. This is the Potter's way, this is God's way when working with us!

Listen to this: **"...so he made it again into another vessel, as it seemed good to the potter to make."**

Throughout the creation process of making this clay vessel, the Potter works with determination and intention, to bring about something that is good in His eyes—not my eyes or anyone else's. What a beautiful piece of celestial information!

In other words, the Potter is not going to settle for any bit of mediocrity. He will work and work and work, until it seems good to Him! The combination of the words, **"it seemed good to..."** literally means to be smooth, straight, or right:agreeable: to His eye.

As I close this first part, I want you to reflect on why sometimes things tend to repeat in our lives, and often more than once or twice. If we are facing the same trial or circumstance, it is probably because we have not learned it the first time! There is a training process taking place in us – we may not understand it – but the Potter has it all figured out!

Trust His judgment: He is not stopping the work in us,

until **"it seems good to..."** Him!

28

Inside the Potter's Heart – Part 2

"Then the word of the Lord came to me, saying: 'O house of Israel, can I not do with you as this potter?'" (Jeremiah 18:6a)

Once someone gets touched by God, the highway to the abundance that one has in God is endless. It is at this place where God desires us to live and abide!

As I have opened up the first part of the Potter's heart, I want to add another part to it, and perhaps one of the most key parts in our development in God.

It is truly one thing for God to desire to do great things in our lives, but altogether a different thing, in us allowing Him to do this very thing inside of us.

I find the story of the Potter and the Clay, which is in Jeremiah 18, to be very practical and prophetic. Obviously, God desires to take us and form us into something He can qualify for the purpose of using our lives to manifest His glory on the earth. This has always been His heart.

Now, things become difficult, when we don't understand the Potter's intent. If we don't see our training in character from God's perspective, we might end up aborting all God desires to do in us. God can desire to do — but we can also stop the flow of what God wants to do. Not allowing Him to work in us will definitely hinder our development and spiritual maturity.

Allowing God To:

1. Transform Our Spirit. First of all, I want to address one of the main areas that I believe God desires to transform in us — this would be our spirit. God's Holy Spirit wants to possess our spirit and empower it so that we may live empowered lives! Too often we are powerless, because we have not allowed God to fill our lives with His Spirit. It is His Spirit that vivifies us! It is His Spirit that reveals the purpose or reason for our existence. All vision comes from the Spirit of God. We must allow God to have His way in us.

2. Transform Our Mind. One of the most precious gifts God could have given us is a mind. When we came into the Kingdom of God, He equipped us with the mind of Christ. He gave us the knowledge of what to do and when to do whatever needed to be done for our everyday life. The more we study the Scriptures, the more we understand the knowledge of God. The more we become students of the knowledge of God, the more we will allow His knowledge to lead us and guide us in every season of our lives. God knows the seasons are changing!

3. Transform Our Emotions. Finally, we must allow God to train us in our emotions. Our emotions are key to what we do. If our emotions are not set in-line with God's emotions, we will not understand what God is feeling. In the case of a trial or test, we might allow our emotions to get the best of us, and we might just whine or complain like little children and never graduate from all that God wants to do in us.

In closing this meditation, allowing God to do all He needs to do in us is really something we must come to grips with. It is not only beneficial to our spiritual development; but it is also a key component to the building of a good foundation for our future purpose in God.

29

A Fight! A Race! A Faith!

"For I am already being poured out as a drink offering, and the time of my departure is at hand. I have fought the good fight, I have finished the race, I have kept the faith. Finally, there is laid up for me the crown of righteousness, which the Lord, the righteous Judge, will give to me on that Day, and not to me only, but also to all who have loved His appearing." (2 Timothy 4:6-8)

In meditating upon the life of the Apostle Paul, one has to be in awe of this man's life — how he lived it with such zeal, strength, passion, and assurance.

In reading all his Epistles, I never felt that Paul was ever complaining or desiring to switch his lot in life with someone else. He understood that all his life had been hand-picked by God, and that he was what he was by the sole grace of God.

As the Apostle Paul comes to the end of his career here on earth, Paul writes his last letter to Timothy. In 2 Timothy 4:6, Paul says that he is already **"being poured out as a drink offering, and the time of [his] departure was at hand."**

Obviously, the Apostle Paul was very aware of what his position and time in jail would mean. He knew time was running out for him, and the end to his calling here on earth was imminent.

It is with this in mind that I want to unfold the following portion of Paul's words:

Paul said, **"I have fought the good fight, I have finished the race, I have kept the faith."**

There are three things that entertained Paul's thoughts as He pursued the heart of God and chased after the will of

God for his own life.

The first thing on his list were these words: **"I have fought the good fight."** What did Paul mean by this? He meant that he was faithful in keeping himself holy and separated for the purpose God had enlisted him for. Was it easy in following Christ? I bet it was not—especially during the times when Paul lived. It must have been a dog fight! In his letter, Paul says, "I have fought the good fight." He didn't cheat God or anyone with anything. It was a good fight!

Secondly, Paul said, **"I have finished my race."** He didn't start something and leave it halfway— no sir! Paul went all out with everything he had; there was not an ounce of mediocrity in this man's blood! If anyone desires to follow hard after the heart of God and fulfill the will of the Father, one must count the cost and finish the race! Don't start and then quit!

Lastly, Paul said, **"I have kept the faith."** It's one thing to go through turmoil and adversity and allow it to make one bitter and hurt; but altogether a different thing, when one clings to the Lord in the most strenuous of situations, and remains humble, broken and submissive to God. Keeping the faith doesn't only mean that you keep coming to church all bitter! It means you keep coming to church with a humble and teachable spirit.

In closing, always be aware that God is working within us. It's not about the externals as much as it is about the internal work of God through His Spirit.

30

Restructure and Reorder! - Part 1

"Now therefore, thus says the Lord, the God of Israel, concerning this city of which you say, 'It shall be delivered into the hand of the king of Babylon by the sword, by the famine, and by the pestilence: Behold, I will gather them out of all countries where I have driven them in My anger, in My fury, and in great wrath; I will bring them back to this place, and I will cause them to dwell safely. They shall be My people, and I will be their God; then I will give them one heart and one way, that they may fear Me forever, for the good of them and their children after them. And I will make an everlasting covenant with them, that I will not turn away from doing them good; but I will put My fear in their hearts so that they will not depart from Me. Yes, I will rejoice over them to do them good, and I will assuredly plant them in this land, with all My heart and with all My soul."

For thus says the Lord: 'Just as I have brought all this great calamity on this people, so I will bring on them all the good that I have promised them.'" (Jeremiah 32:36-42)

When reading the book of Jeremiah, I have always felt the sense that this book was instructional for anyone who desires to know God's heart in a deeper way. For anyone who wants to know and understand the wisdom, heart and mind of God — the book of Jeremiah is a beautiful layout of all this and then some.

His ministry of brokenness and how Jeremiah allowed the Lord Jehovah to use him was such an honoring ministry. Though not an easy task, Jeremiah became the voice of God during a time when Judah was in major rebellion against God.

Jeremiah would hear the Lord's heart and prophesy it to the leadership of Judah. As it is with all rebellious spirits, the leadership didn't want to hear it much less receive it! The king was so defiant against God and His word that

Jeremiah would end up in jail because of it. Definitely not a ministry for the weak in heart.

The Discipline of the Lord

Obviously, the Lord was not going to allow anyone to get away with anything that was not pleasing to Him. Judgment was imminent. The Lord was not pleased at all, and His discipline was about to hit Judah like a tsunami. This is how Babylon got tapped on the shoulder to come and be a tool of discipline and fulfill God's wishes.

I have heard many servants of the Lord speak of coming judgment for years; they speak of how the Lord will punish this or that, him or her, because of this or that! When I hear my dear brothers or sisters prophesy judgment, my heart breaks because they do it with such anger and a bitterness in their soul. I personally don't think the Lord feels exactly that way!

I think most people who are in touch with God's heart

don't prophesy like that.   God's heart is not for destruction upon His people, but rather a discipline. Listen to what Proverbs 3:12 says, "…because the Lord disciplines those he loves, as a father the son he delights in."

Let's look at the word discipline for a bit. The word discipline in the Hebrew means, "to correct."

The picture I have discovered in the Lord's heart when disciplining His people is one of correction. Like a father telling his son with a nourishing spirit, "This is not the way you do this — do it this way!" And in loving judgment, the son stands corrected in the matter.

God doesn't want to spank the daylights out of anyone, but in loving judgment he seeks to bring them up to the place that pleases Him! As Romans 2:4 says, "…it is the goodness of the Lord that leads man to repentance," not his anger!

When the Lord allowed Babylon to take them captive for

seventy years, it wasn't to get even with them, destroy them, or be a mean God to them. No sir! I believe God had a bigger vision for His people: To bring them to a greater reality of who He is and what plans He had for them.

We really don't appreciate something until we lose it! Judah lost their freedom when God (through the Babylonian army) had to bring them under captivity (note: not bondage) to teach them a great lesson for all of us to see! This was the beginning of reordering for Judah.

31

Restructure and Reorder! - Part 2

"For thus says the Lord: 'Just as I have brought all this great calamity on this people, so I will bring on them all the good that I have promised them.'" (Jeremiah 32:42)

What a tremendous change of events happened to Judah. Once in freedom and now under Babylonian captivity.

One can judge and say, **"God is not compassionate and merciful. He is mad, and He is going to punish His people for their idolatry and unfaithfulness to Him!"**

Yet, this statement could not be further from the truth.

Does one really think that God is into annihilating His people? I think not. But I do believe God allows things to fall apart and break at times. Why? Because of His intent to reorder our lives to the place where it will bring Him the greatest glory.

Too often I have seen the Lord deal with our own personal lives in ways that few can understand. People will look from the outside and judge, while others will conclude that something has seen its last days.

God Is Always Working!

all the chaos, God is working in the midst of it! He did it in the life of most of His chosen servants. He did with Abraham, Jacob, Job, David, Jeremiah, Jesus Christ, Peter, the Apostle Paul, and countless others.

Just because things are "shut down" for a season, it doesn't mean that the game is over. No sir! I believe that God does send us [His servants,] into spiritual dungeons and deserts for seasons at a time. Granted, some seasons are longer than others; yet, the intent of God is to reorder our lives and align it with His will and purpose!

Captivity Is Not the Same as Bondage!

When the Lord had the Babylonian empire come after His people in Judah, it was to teach them a great lesson. Once the lesson would be learned, God would be sending them back home where God had promised them land.

The Lord wasn't trying to destroy them; He was trying to bring them to higher ground!

When someone is in the confines of bondage, it brings discouragement and desperation with no answer in sight. There is an overwhelming sensation of darkness and the sense that there is no door and now way out to escape! Have you experienced this?

Captivity is a lot different. God had Judah in captivity for seventy years. It was His intent to keep them under watch by the Babylonian Empire so that God's people would appreciate and see all that they had aborted and discarded.

When God's heart reached satisfaction and the lesson had been learned, God released them back into the land.

God will never waste an opportunity to do great things in our lives. He will do all that is within His power to get us to the mountain— to the place of deeper intimacy and revelation.

32

Learn to Count the Cost!

"For which of you, intending to build a tower, does not sit down first and count the cost, whether he has enough to finish it—lest, after he has laid the foundation, and is not able to finish, all who see it begin to mock him, saying, 'This man began to build and was not able to finish.'" (Luke 14:27-30)

Near the place where my ministry base is, there is a huge house and to be more exact, I think its original blueprint was for it to be a mansion of some sort. It is enormous! Yet at the same time, the house is empty, it's vacant. No one lives there because the house was never completed or finished. Not from the outside and not from the inside. What a testimony wouldn't you say?!

Building with Wisdom!

In following God, Jesus made it pretty plain. He shared His heart with some who were daring to follow Him and become His disciples. He told them that it would not be easy; that it would cost them everything - if they truly desired to follow Him to the end.

The Lord's heart here was given for the sole purpose to prevent embarrassment to those who desired to follow Him. He didn't want anyone, over-committing to His cause with many emotional promises, empty words and fleshly expressions of service. He knew the road would not be easy for anyone who desired to follow, and He totally understood that times would get tough and extremely inconvenient!

Not Able to Finish!

Too often people who come to Christ think that just because they have made a decision to follow Him with their whole hearts, that the road to building a great life will be as easy as 1, 2, 3. If any Bible teacher ever tells you that, they are lying to you!

It is correct to understand that the foundation is the beginning of a house. To build a foundation for your life in Christ is most definitely the best choice you will ever make in this life. As valuable as a great foundation is, the foundation is only the first step to the building. There is yet a frame that must be build on it, walls, a roof, windows and doors.

When one desires to pursue greatness, one must "budget in" the whole cost, not just the initial registration fee. When building a house, obviously the foundation is an expensive part of the whole project. If you only have $25,000.00 saved or borrowed for the construction of your house and the foundation is that much, then when will the framing go up? When will the walls be built or the windows and doors placed?

Jesus is saying to us who are His followers, "Sit down first and count the cost, and evaluate whether [there is] enough to finish it." Surely, the Lord doesn't want anybody embarrassed or ridiculed for their lack of planning and for making unwise decisions.

33

Awake the Christ In You!

Why are you cast down, O my soul?
And why are you disquieted within me?
Hope in God;
For I shall yet praise Him,
The help of my countenance and my God." (Psalm 43:5)

What a Psalm! Actually, the writer of this song is expressing an emotion that is all too common in the human soul — I am speaking of the pain in the soul when it is out of harmony with God for whatever reason that might be.

The songwriter poses the question, **"Why are you cast down, O my soul?"** And then again, poses another question, **"And why are you disquieted within me?"** The word disquieted in the original manuscript mean growl, roar, to be boisterous.

What the songwriter is in essence saying is this, "Why am I disturbed within me? What is this feeling that has me roaring, growling deep inside? Why do I feel like there is a storm blowing in my inward parts?"

This Psalm brings me to a story in the New Testament in the book of Mark chapter 4:35 as the disciples went along for a ride with Jesus in a boat: **"On the same day, when evening had come, He said to them, 'Let us cross over to the other side.' Now when they had left the multitude, they took Him along in the boat as He was. And other little boats were also with Him. And a great windstorm arose, and the waves beat into the boat, so that it was already filling. But He was in the stern, asleep on a pillow. And they awoke Him and said to Him, 'Teacher, do You not care that we are perishing?' Then He arose and rebuked the wind, and said to the sea, 'Peace, be still!' And the wind ceased and there was a great calm. But He said to them, 'Why are you so fearful? How is it that you have no faith?' And they feared exceedingly, and said to one another, 'Who can this be, that even the wind and the sea obey Him!'"**

In this particular story, the disciples of Jesus were being

taken to the other side to minister and while Jesus slept, a boisterous storm came and shook the boat and the disciples as well.

The storm was so powerful that the disciples began to come under the power of fear. They truly felt that they had seen their last boat ride!

Finally, they mustered enough courage to wake up the Lord and in His usual fashion, Jesus took authority and quieted the storm!

What shook the disciples? What made them fear? What brought about a boisterous spirit within them? Nothing more than a boisterous storm! This is always the case.

When faith leaves, fear comes!

The key to living a victorious life has not changed. We tend to change, but the way God ministers to us, never does!

The Psalmist says after posing all the questions, **"Hope in God!"** The word hope means to wait or await. All our answers are found in waiting upon the Lord. Wait for His voice; wait for His counsel; wait for His power; wait for His prompting; wait for His peace!

The Psalmist tells his own soul, **"Wait on God!"**

We would benefit greatly if we can enter in and adapt this mindset, the mindset of the songwriter, the mindset of God!

34

Now Faith Is!

"Now faith is the substance of things hoped for, the evidence of things not seen." (Hebrews 11:1)

Hebrews 11 in the Bible, otherwise known as the chapter of faith is a pretty powerful chapter on the great things God has done through a man or woman of faith. One would think that walking by faith is really as easy as 1, 2, 3.

Blind Faith

Sometimes I have seen people walk with God with blind faith. Not knowing, not caring, and not worried, if things will turn out fine in their everyday life. There are some who walk this way and to be honest with you, it has worked out for some.

When it comes to blind faith, I define this, as someone who walks inside the parameters of God's mercy. By all standards, they should not do well, because of the obvious violation of godly laws, but because of God's mercy, things work out! I don't understand — but it seems to work for some.

Real Faith

Now real faith to me, seems to be something I can grasp with my mind and my heart. Real faith is something that comes from the Lord into the human heart and is processed by the mind. It is God speaking or allowing the human vessel excess into God's spiritual realm in a real way, in a deeper way!

Real faith is a quickening faith that comes into the human heart with information that was not present before. It is a revelatory thought that changes, provokes, and quickens the individual with a "breath of fresh air."

Have you ever been so down and out for whatever reason and someone came in to your life with "a word" that seemed like a "breath of fresh air?" This is exactly what real faith is! It's a word from heaven understood by the inner deep within you.

Prophetic Pictures

In learning to hear God with my own life, I have learned that God speaks loud and clear through prophetic pictures or visual ideas and concepts. He will often give me a dream or a vision that can be spiritually processed and understood.

Once your spirit-man [aka, inner-man,] acknowledges it's God by a subtle and deep confirmation within you, the acceptance of that, is literally, real faith kicking in. Once real faith kicks in, walk on it and do exactly as the picture appeared to you in the vision, dream or word.

35

The God-Pleasers: A Note of Quality

By faith Enoch was taken away so that he did not see death, "and was not found, because God had taken him"; for before he was taken he had this testimony that he pleased God." (Hebrews 11:5)

Wow! Enoch was taken away so that he did not see death. How does a man walk above and beyond death (God's last enemy)? The Scripture bears it out: **"...he pleased God." What does it mean, "...he pleased God?"**

I want to break down some definitions that will allow us to see a deeper revelation of what it means to walk in the realm of Enoch. That realm where death can't touch you.

First of all, let's look at the definition. The word of God says in Hebrews 11:5 that Enoch "pleased" God. How does a common man or woman do this? To please means to be"content" or "acceptable." It means that in the Christian walk, one pursues this idea and makes it his or her goal — to please God!

It's the motive of wanting to do this with every great desire in you. To have the permission of God in all that you do, so that He is willing to bless and reward you with every good thing.

The Realm of Enoch

The realm in which Enoch walked, is a prophetic picture of where every believer can potentially enter into. It's a place that is focused on the face of God. The believer is attentive to God's facial expressions as he beholds Him.

With every move, an expression is made: Either God will smile expressing His joy over you or God will frown at the displeasure of us walking outside of His will.

When one enters this walk with the motive of desiring to be in good standing with God, this elevates the man or woman to a higher realm in God. The ability to see the invisible and appropriate God's heart becomes possible and easier to grasp.

It is at this spiritual state that death loses its grip on you because it can't touch anything that is of God. Death might claim your body but not your soaring spirit!

36

Who Built & Made Your House?

"By faith Abraham obeyed when he was called to go out to the place which he would receive as an inheritance. And he went out, not knowing where he was going. By faith he dwelt in the land of promise as in a foreign country, dwelling in tents with Isaac and Jacob, the heirs with him of the same promise; for he waited for the city which has foundations, whose builder and maker is God." (Hebrews 11:8-10)

The idea that one can make their own kingdom and live in it is the biggest lie sold to humanity from the beginning of time. The devil (the serpent) in Eden did this. He sold a house to Eve and Adam; he told them that they could be just like God and they bought this house (this idea) that brought nothing but death and disgrace!

Many today are building and making their own ideas of

how life could or should be. I believe that we do have a responsibility to build and make our house (life), but God must precede the idea — in other words, the idea must come from God first, then we build according to His pattern.

When Living in a Tent is Not a Bad Idea!
"By faith he dwelt in the land of promise as in a foreign country, dwelling in tents..."

If you take this idea and apply it to modern times, it would make little sense to our Western culture and society. No one desires to live in a tent!

The only time a tent would be appropriate in our western world would be if we had no other place to live, or if we went on a camping trip.

Now, a tent is a house made out of canvas or animal skins without a solid foundation. Solidifying a tent with a solid foundation underneath it would mean that the tent would not have the ability to move to another location.

Why wouldn't Abraham build a foundation [signifying a permanent address]? Because a tent wasn't home for him! Abraham was "waiting" for a city whose builder and maker was God. He was looking for something else that God had promised. You see a tent was not where Abraham's heart was set it was only temporary.

We can't afford to make "the temporary" become "the permanent." If we do this, we will trap ourselves in our own dream. It is better to build a tent when you know that God has greater things for you than to settle for second best.

When Your Heart Sees It — You Will Know!

As you wait upon the Lord for guidance and direction for your steps, you will process everything around you. You will be on the lookout, but none of those things will move your heart to build a foundation.

Then it will happen: Your heart will see it! Your hands will reach for it; your heart will explode with joy, and your resources will unveil themselves supernaturally from an unseen treasure!

37

Why Hearing God Has Not Been Happening to You!

"See that you do not refuse Him who speaks." (Hebrews 12:25)

Walking with the Lord is really and truly an act of faith. One can't walk with God if he can't believe in God's laws and apply them to their daily lives. One must believe enough to take God at His holy word and allow that "word" to be a compass of sorts.

Often, I hear people say to me, "Pastor, God never talks to me." Or "Why is it that I can't hear God say anything to me?"

This is a common issue among Christ's followers, but why?

Here's what I believe is the culprit to the lack of hearing or listening to God. There might be more culprits or obstacles that one can attempt to blame for their lack of hearing God — but here's some I have experienced.

1. Not really looking for God's direction. I have been around many believers in my short walk with God, and I have heard many make the noble plea of, "I really need a touch from God." It is sincere, it is an honest plea and even the tears to go with it. Yet deep within their heart, in their inner man, they really don't want to hear God. They have a struggle, and they really don't want to be free from it. The fact is this: God is speaking, but it is not what they want to hear. God is speaking of the issue of struggle; they are wanting another type of "word." They want to talk about another subject all the while, God wants to talk about the thing that has them trapped!

2. Lack of Humility. I have seen in my seeking of God's face, that often when I can't hear God — it is not because He doesn't speak to me; it has to do with my heart

condition. My heart might be "set" on a wayward way and not broken, contrite or humble enough, making it not receptive to God's divine plan. There may be a tad of rebellion that we are holding on to— a sense of, "I'm right, and I've always been right." This is not a good attitude to approach God's throne with. God will not have it and will withhold the revelation for another time.

3. A Biased Opinion. Too often believers come to God with a mind already made up. They already know what they want and need; no one is going to deter them from their desired end. God will never fight with a man who has already made up his mind. It is not that God doesn't speak to them; it's more like, God knows that you will not listen to Him in the pursuit of what you want! When one comes to God, one must come with an open unbiased heart and mind.

Never think that God is not speaking to any of us; He is speaking and obviously more than we know. Make sure that as you approach the throne room of grace in prayer, you come believing, broken, contrite, and with an unbiased heart!

38

The Silent War Within!

"Where do wars and fights come from among you? Do they not come from your desires for pleasure that war in your members? You lust and do not have. You murder and covet and cannot obtain. You fight and war. Yet you do not have because you do not ask. You ask and do not receive, because you ask amiss, that you may spend it on your pleasures. Adulterers and adulteresses! Do you not know that friendship with the world is enmity with God? Whoever therefore wants to be a friend of the world makes himself an enemy of God. Or do you think that the Scripture says in vain, "The Spirit who dwells in us yearns jealously?" (James 4:1-5)

This morning meditation was truly out of this world for me — let me share it with you:

The thing in question is and for the most part, has been the troubled-feeling we often feel when things are not good with us, around us, or in us. You know what I am talking about — that awful feeling of unsettledness, almost as if there is a pulling of arguments within you to be well or at peace.

What is the Fighting All About?

The fight is usually felt deep within your spiritual being. Every fight starts at the well of self. The carnal [fleshly, worldly, old-natured, selfish] part of you is attempting to "inch" its way into your God-given spiritual-valued system of Godly principles and attempting to manipulate the ways of God.

The struggle is silent. The manipulation is subtle. But the Spirit of God has a radar like no other. It picks up the countering of thoughts, values, principles, imparted into your heart by God's Spirit. Anything that goes against God's principles in you, will be rapidly detected, and the war will be on!

You can ask a brother or a sister: Why are you downcast? Why are you discouraged? I guarantee you that most of the time, it will be because they are in a silent war with the flesh. Their Spirit longs to soar, but the fleshly nature has other plans!

Why the Struggle is a Good Sign of Life

When one is not happy with himself or herself, one tends to get discouraged. When our lives are not in harmony with God's agenda, or when our life is feeling unhappy with the bad choices we have made – this is a good sign of life.

The Scripture says, **"The Spirit who dwells in us yearns jealously?"** This means that God's Holy Spirit is alive in us and fighting within us for territory to be gained and conquered for Jesus' sake! The discouragement we feel, is a sign that a battle is going on and we must continue to take a hold of the hem of His garment until the battle is won.

The greater the discouragement, the greater the fight! The greater the sadness and loneliness and despair that we feel — the greater the power of Christ within us to fight to obtain harmony with God!

Lacking Peace?

When one is not at peace for whatever reason, know that disharmony with God's design for you has come. The flesh makes its attempt to deter you from God's perfect plan for you, but God's Spirit is also letting you know that things are not ok, and that you need to make the necessary adjustments (spiritually speaking) to the situation at hand. Once you align with God's design — His sweet and perfect peace will come upon you and overtake you.

39

Recognition!

"Now behold, two of them were traveling that same day to a village called Emmaus, which was seven miles from Jerusalem. And they talked together of all these things which had happened. So it was, while they conversed and reasoned, that Jesus Himself drew near and went with them. But their eyes were restrained, so that they did not know Him." (Luke 24:13-16)

How many times has it happened in your life that you were in the midst of "turbulent times," and could not really understand why all the upheaval? You looked and searched all around you, but all to no effect - nothing made sense.

It is usually at these times that friends come along and provide some kind of comfort and sympathy, but after they leave your presence, you go back to the same old feeling of lost-ness and discouragement. Do you know what I'm talking about?

This emotion and experience will continue to take place many more times in our lifetime. Why does it happen? I don't really know. But here is what I have learned in my short time of walking with Jesus...

When All Is in Question

Take for example the life of the two followers of Jesus on the road to Emmaus:

Jesus had been crucified, and all that had been promised and all that had been spoken about the kingdom, all of it, was now in question.

After leaving all their careers, jobs, and everything they had to follow Christ, these servants were now left with no tangible promise in sight. Can you imagine the state of mind? Can you relate?

As they walked back to the town of Emmaus and talked about all that had taken place in the last few days, they were torn and could not explain how things could end up in such a way!

Human Reasoning

The Scripture goes on to say, **"So it was, while they conversed and reasoned, that Jesus Himself drew near and went with them."**

I don't know a lot about a lot of things, but one thing I know: The more I converse with myself or with someone, the more I enter into some type of reasoning. Holy Spirit reasoning is one thing, but human reasoning [Gr. to examine; or discuss] can get us into a lot of trouble. To know the difference is key to coming out of turmoil and into a peaceful state.

After reasoning for some time, Jesus decides to show up in the midst of their confused conversation. As Jesus joins the conversation, He said to them, **"What kind of conver-**

sation is this that you have with one another as you walk and are sad?"

Sadness is a sign that things are not in order in one's heart. A piece of information is missing from one's heart and mind and it is challenging us to seek and search out the matter. Jesus knew that about them — that is why He shows up in a different form.

The Lord had restrained their eyes from seeing Him, and they were not able to recognize Him— but the Lord who never sleeps or slumbers, was very present to help [see Psalm 121: 1-5.]

Jesus Unveils Himself

After having a lengthy conversation about the events with this stranger (Jesus), the men asked Jesus to stay the night because it was already late. Jesus opted to stay, and this is what happened: **"Now it came to pass, as He sat at the table with them, that He took bread, blessed and broke it, and gave it to them. Then their eyes were opened and**

they knew Him; and He vanished from their sight. And they said to one another, "Did not our heart burn within us while He talked with us on the road, and while He opened the Scriptures to us?" (Luke 24:30-32)

Only when we get into His presence and recognize Him, only then, will we complete the puzzle. Only then, will our circumstances make sense. Once Jesus appears, the mystery is taken away!

Let us draw near and stay in His presence awhile; let all our confusion melt like wax in the presence of the Lord!

40

Positioned for Greatness!

'Whom are you like in your greatness?
Indeed Assyria was a cedar in Lebanon,
With fine branches that shaded the forest,
And of high stature;
And its top was among the thick boughs.
The waters made it grow;
Underground waters gave it height.
'Thus it was beautiful in greatness and in the length of its branches,
Because its roots reached to abundant waters." (Ezekiel 31:2-4, 7)

Meditating upon the book of Ezekiel this morning, I came across a principle so powerful and so true. Let me share my thoughts on it with you...

Where Does Growth Come From?

Being a person who likes to plant and see plants grow and mature, I have always taken note that wherever there is moisture, plants tend to be healthier. Not only do they stay healthy in color, but also in growth.

I do believe that fruitfulness is contingent upon good soil and proper watering. I know that by first-hand experience.

Just as it is in the natural world, so it is in the spiritual. If one doesn't water their spirit and soul, one will dry up. The discernment [ability to distinguish between right and wrong] will be clouded, the emotions will be only soulish, and common sense will be selfish more than what God truly desires.

Planted by the Rivers...

"Blessed is the man

Who walks not in the counsel of the ungodly,
Nor stands in the path of sinners,
Nor sits in the seat of the scornful;
But his delight is in the law of the Lord,
And in His law he meditates day and night.
He shall be like a tree
Planted by the rivers of water,
That brings forth its fruit in its season,
Whose leaf also shall not wither;
And whatever he does shall prosper." (Psalm 1:1-3)

In this Psalm, we read about this tree being planted by rivers. Naturally, fruit will come forth in its season, the leaves stay beautiful and they don't wither – and prosperity seems to just follow this beautiful tree!

The tree doesn't need to look for prosperity, it needs to be planted near water! Prosperity comes because of where it is planted — not because of its desire to have fruit and or not have withering leaves!

Prosperity comes because of where tree is positioned, not because of the tree's desire! Just listen to the principle: **"Thus it was beautiful in greatness and in the length of its branches, because its roots reached to abundant waters."** (Ezekiel 31:7)

Position Yourself for Greatness!

If there is a key element that we should seriously work on — it should be our positioning.

If we want better health, we will position ourselves into a good eating plan and exercise program. If we want a better position financially, we will develop a good stewardship program and apply the principles that enhance our personal situation, and if we want to strengthen our spiritual vitality, then a good disciplined personal prayer life and Bible meditation will begin the process.

Remember: Being planted by the rivers is the key to a life of fruitfulness!

41

His Beautiful Face!

**"The Lord is good to those who wait for Him,
To the soul who seeks Him.
It is good that one should hope and wait quietly
For the salvation of the Lord."** (Lamentations 3:25, 26)

I have noticed something very valuable about the different types of adversities that man is dealt in his daily life. What I have perceived is how tests have a way of teaching each individual countless and important lessons about themselves.

As much as one would love to shift the blame on the circumstances at hand, the mature person will always look to the face of God for clarity. Not too many in our day are teaching this. There are countless ministries who teach the opposite to this.

Some are quick to judge the situation and start blaming outside forces (such as people, institutions, even Satan gets a kick in his behind), for all the pain and suffering they go through.

The mature believer thinks very differently and pursues the One who can change everything!

In the Scripture written as our text, I learned that the word good in Hebrew, means beautiful. In other words, the Scripture can also read like this: "The Lord is beautiful to those who wait for Him, to the soul who seeks Him."

The church of our day understands very little about the beauty behind waiting on God.

People focus more on self than they do on what God really desires. For people who are not into "waiting," on God, life seems like a big mystery. Every circumstance is dreadful — so it is easier to complain and whine, rather than wait and receive revelation from the heart of God!

Jeremiah the Prophet, the author of the Book of Lamentations, saw waiting upon the Lord as a thing of beauty.

He was moved by the heart of God— he wept incessantly because of the sin which would bring judgment upon God's people. Jeremiah saw the beauty of God; he knew that God would always give favor to those who would favor Him. Yet, no one stirred their hearts to go after God's heart. Judgment was inevitable after this.

Trying hard to overcome adversity in our own strength is never easy. It's an endless pursuit to find peace and significance. Many have trod that road one too many times, only to find out that it's impossible to have peace when God is not involved.

Jeremiah saw the value of waiting upon God, because He saw the beauty behind the secret. It was beauty that attracted him to this arduous work of seeking God in the secret place.

Many are looking for answers; Jeremiah was looking for

God's beautiful face!

Let us learn to find His beautiful face as we wait upon Him!

42

You Must Know - So Pray Until You Do!

"Now when much time had been spent, and sailing was now dangerous because the Fast was already over, Paul advised them, saying, Men, I perceive that this voyage will end with disaster and much loss, not only of the cargo and ship, but also our lives.' Nevertheless the centurion was more persuaded by the helmsman and the owner of the ship than by the things spoken by Paul." (Acts 27:9-11)

While meditating upon this particular story in the book of Acts chapter 27, I discovered a powerful principle. I would love to share with you this truth.

Remember that at this time, the Apostle Paul was now a prisoner and was on his way to Rome to see Caesar. Along with another two-hundred plus men, they set sail to their destination.

Paul, an Intuitive Prophetic Man

It was during this time that the Apostle Paul spoke some very wise words. I don't know if he just had an intuition, inclination, or if God was prophetically speaking to him. Whatever was the case, the Apostle Paul advised the leaders of the ship, **"Men, I perceive that this voyage will end with disaster and much loss, not only of the cargo and ship, but also our lives."** Paul didn't feel good about the trip, and since he was perhaps the only man in touch with God, he voiced his feelings.

We must always be attentive to the prophetic voice of God; it is not normal to sense things "out of the blue." I believe God speaks this way. He allows us to feel and to sense what He is about to do in our lives.

The Danger of Not Listening to the Counsel of God

Please notice: As good as the advice from Paul was, the Scripture says, **"Nevertheless the centurion was more persuaded by the helmsman and the owner of the ship than what by the things spoken by Paul."**

I do believe that God always speaks loud and clear. And as usual, it is the human vessel who struggles with God's intent. It is us human beings who often "drop the ball," and we don't hear God speaking to our situation.

Basing Matters on Common Sense

For natural people, this usually works out pretty well for the majority of the time. Human calculations have their place, but there is a greater calling than this.... it's called the spirit-filled life!

People who walk under the leadership of the Spirit, operate with a whole new set of faculties. They listen, process and act differently than the natural man. They live in the world of the supernatural sustained by the faith of God in them.

It is obvious, by reading the story, that the leaders of the ship based their decision on sailing at that time, based on the favorable circumstances at hand. The helmsman and the owner were on the same page, but Paul wasn't! The natural man saw the profit – the spiritual man saw the danger!

Always Check with Heaven Before Making a Move!

The story goes on to say that they were hit hard by a storm for about fourteen days. They lost the cargo, the nearly lost the ship, and if it had not been for the mercy of God, all of the people on board, would have died.

Thank God for the spiritual man onboard!

Yes, Paul had a visitation from an angel on one of the darkest nights. After receiving word from God, Paul revealed this: **"And now I urge you to take heart, for there will be** no loss of life among you, but only of the ship. For there stood by me this night an angel of the God to whom I belong and whom I serve, saying, 'Do not be afraid, Paul; you must be brought before Caesar; and indeed God has granted you all those who sail with you.' Therefore, take heart, men, for I believe God that it will be just as it was told me." (Acts 27:22-25)

This story serves us as a great lesson on waiting upon the Lord for His timing, direction, and protection. Let us develop and cultivate this kind of life; a life of godly discernment.

43

The Lord of Every Secret! - Part 1

Daniel answered and said:
"Blessed be the name of God forever and ever,
For wisdom and might are His.
And He changes the times and the seasons;
He removes kings and raises up kings;
He gives wisdom to the wise
And knowledge to those who have understanding.
He reveals deep and secret things;
He knows what is in the darkness,
And light dwells with Him." (Daniel 2:20-22)

Aren't you glad for your GPS system or your Google Maps App? I know I am very thankful and forever grateful for it. I really think that those inventions are perhaps some of the most useful items of all time. I can tell you how many times I have said, "I'm so thankful for this gadget!"

What is a GPS, what does it stand for? Here's the definition: The Global Positioning System (GPS) is a space-based navigation system that provides location and time information in all weather conditions, anywhere on or near the Earth where there is an unobstructed line of sight to four or more GPS satellites. The system provides critical capabilities to military, civil, and commercial users around the world.

What is Google Maps? Google Maps is a web mapping service developed by Google. It offers satellite imagery, aerial photography, street maps, 360° panoramic views of streets, real-time traffic conditions, and route planning for traveling by foot, car, bicycle and air, or even public transportation.

There is another form of mapping— it's God's supernatural way of leading us in our daily lives. Through His Spirit, He provides accurate leadership and brings us to places that will serve us, help us and bring us into dimensions that will bring Him greater glory!

Here is a fact: God didn't leave us in the world so we could be lost, uneasy, and worried about tomorrow. No way, no how!

God provided us with everything we needed to get from one point in our lives to another. He provided a highway to drive on; He made a bridge for us to cross huge open valleys and rivers, and He even provided a mapping system to guide us every inch of the way — till we reach His destination for us!

How can anyone lose by following God's mapping devices?

God of Wisdom and Might!

In the Scripture I used here, Daniel speaks of God's character and qualities. He says that wisdom and might are God's. He knows everything about anything created. It's really hard to miss any mark or desired destination when you have communication with the Holy Spirit.

Seasons of Learning

Daniel continues and says that God **"changes the times and the seasons."** Amazing!

In our own personal lives, we face many obstacles and situations. We can call them seasons of learning. During these seasons, many things change. We are constantly transitioning. We go from a hard place to a harder place; sometimes we go from an extreme situation to an easier one and we wonder, "How did this happen?" God is Lord of the seasons! That is how.

If we stay in tune with our mapping device (the Holy Spirit), we will discover God's intent for allowing us to go through such changes.

Keep Clinging!

In my heart of hearts, I would love to understand everything that surrounds me on a daily basis, but all too often, God hides some of those things from me. It almost seems as if God wants me to continue clinging on to the hem of His garment, for every move I make in my life!

Let us learn that God has our lives in the palm of His hand and that He desires to take us all the way to our destination.

44

The Lord of Every Secret! - Part 2

"He removes kings and raises up kings;
He gives wisdom to the wise
And knowledge to those who have understanding."
(Daniel 2:21)

He Removes and Raises

As we follow Him and allow ourselves to become daily learners of God's ways, we will discover that God often removes and raises significant things that surround us. Whether it be people or situations, God makes sure that we will learn from it.

It is not an easy thing to keep up with all that God is doing, so humility on our part, must be the order of the day. He must have the preeminence! He must be first.

For all the changes that are surrounding you and I, God is present. He is not sleeping and slumbering. He is right there with us. He is always ready to download wisdom and knowledge as needed. He invites us to come boldly to the throne and ask for whatever it is that we are in need of. What are you going to do with a God like this? So big and beautiful!

The Spirit of Revelation

"He reveals deep and secret things;
He knows what is in the darkness,
And light dwells with Him." (Daniel 2:22)

One of the most powerful and yet mysterious ways of God, in my opinion, is how He opens our eyes to see things that are hidden; things that are under the ground, sea, or in the constellations. He pulls things out of thin air and speaks life to them, and they are created. Created just for me!

As I said on my last meditation, "God didn't leave us in the world so we could be lost, uneasy and worried about tomorrow. No way, no how!

God provided us with everything we needed to get from one point in our lives to another. He provided a highway to drive on; He made a bridge for us to cross huge open valleys and rivers, and He even provided a mapping system to guide us every inch of the way — till we reach His destination for us!"

Let me show you what I mean as you face your circumstance, your crisis, your adversity:

Abraham & Sarah God has made this couple a promise that a son would be born to them when they were about seventy-five years of age. Twenty-five years had now passed and still no baby. Where was God in all this? Was He playing "hide and seek?"

When the season was right, God gave them a son, and they called him Isaac. As impossible as this appeared, God made it happen! God made a way where there was no way!

Moses and God's Children   When Moses was leading God's people out of Egypt, it happened that they got stuck. Pharaoh in hot pursuit of them and with the Red Sea in front of them; there was nowhere to turn but to God in prayer. As Moses cried out to God: **"...The Lord said to Moses, "Why do you cry to Me? Tell the children of Israel to go forward. But lift up your rod and stretch out your hand over the sea and divide it. And the children of Israel shall go on dry ground through the midst of the sea."** (Exodus 14:13-16)

What Moses couldn't see, was that there was a highway under the Red Sea! Once Moses obeyed, the highway came up, and God's people were delivered.

These are the examples of, **"He knows what is in the darkness."** God knows all the back ways, secret ways, hidden ways, all of them. Nothing is hidden from Him. All the secrets are with Him.

If you are facing an impossible situation in your life today, call upon the Lord and let Him show you where your secret highway is – God is still in the deliverance business!

45

I Alone Saw the Vision!

"And I, Daniel, alone saw the vision, for the men who were with me did not see the vision; but a great terror fell upon them, so that they fled to hide themselves. Therefore I was left alone when I saw this great vision, and no strength remained in me; for my vigor was turned to frailty in me, and I retained no strength. Yet I heard the sound of his words; and while I heard the sound of his words I was in a deep sleep on my face, with my face to the ground. Suddenly, a hand touched me, which made me tremble on my knees and on the palms of my hands. And he said to me, 'O Daniel, man greatly beloved, understand the words that I speak to you, and stand upright, for I have now been sent to you.' While he was speaking this word to me, I stood trembling." (Daniel 10:7-11)

And I, Daniel, Alone!

One of the things that I have personally experienced in my walk with God has been this one thing about vision. Visions, in my experience, have always been given by the Lord directly into my spirit-man; this seed will germinate in my heart and mind until faith ignites it and action is taken. The outward manifestation of God's vision will then be seen by those around me.

Apparently, Daniel was the only one who saw this vision. God could have shown it to the other guys chose not to. Why not? I lean to the belief that God speaks important matters to people who are in tune with His heart. Daniel was this type of man. Daniel was a man who wanted God's purposes to be carried out on the earth; he had that kind of heart and longing!

Left with No Strength

It is interesting to note that when a vision from God touches you, it does something to you. It tends to shake you to the very core of your being. Powerful visions from the Lord have a way of making you feel inadequate and powerless; it gives you the sense that without God, you can't do it!

Daniel felt powerless and frail when he experienced this vision.

Vigor Turned to Frailty

Anything that is celestial — at least in my experience, seems to always leave me feeling frail and wondering how this vision will come to pass. It leaves me wondering if I will be able to carry it out, if I will be able to see it manifest. I question my resources, strength, emotions, and abilities.

Cultivate It!

After I have received a vision from God, all I can do is cultivate it by lending myself more to God's direction and wisdom. One must stay quiet before the Lord and attentive to every move He makes.

My spiritual antennas are usually tuned to the highest level and are paying attention to all that can potentially add or subtract to all that God has promised. Making right choices according to God's will is a must if the vision will survive the process of incubation.

Once I have done all I know to do, I wait upon the Lord for His continual direction and manifestation.

46

God Hates This!

"Yet I am the Lord your God
Ever since the land of Egypt,
And you shall know no God but Me;
For there is no savior besides Me.
I knew you in the wilderness,
In the land of great drought.
When they had pasture, they were filled;
They were filled and their heart was exalted;
Therefore they forgot Me." (Hosea 13:4-6)

I was meditating on one of the most valuable principles that God taught His children, and perhaps one of the closest to His heart. He has also left this principle for us His church — to learn it and to walk in it.

In the first part of the Scripture mentioned above, God

doesn't hide the fact that He desires to be number one and have the preeminence among His people Israel. He says, "And you shall know no God but Me; for there is no savior besides Me."

To go against this piece of revelation, to challenge the mind of God in His wisdom, would not be a good thing for Israel or even us His church.   As servants of King Jesus, remember, God is to be first in all things, now and always!

Once we understand this, we can move on to other principles and laws of God for us.

Too Blessed or Lack of Character?

It is apparent that God walked with His people through and through; He was there at every turning point. He was there at every crisis. He was there when they had no one to defend them; and yes, He was there to see them come out of many distressing experiences. We can honestly say, 'God kept His faithfulness going!'

Now, the people of Israel experienced some "wilderness" experiences. They were challenged, and they were torn and tested, yet the Lord healed them and brought them through.

Once they were established, the people of Israel found pasture [blessings] — and they enjoyed every bit of it. Once they found these blessings, the Scripture goes on to say that they "were filled" and their hearts became filled with pride. Listen: **"They were filled and their heart was exalted; Therefore they forgot Me."**

Why is pride such a horrible thing? Well for one, God hates it! Also, pride is really a statement made which says, "I am self-sufficient in myself; I don't need God or anyone to help me along. I can figure life out all by myself."

Nothing is more damning than a heart that lifts itself against the Lord! God help us all. Once pride takes over, God is out of our personal picture.

The Scripture says that after their hearts were filled with pride, they forgot God. This should not come as a surprise to any one of us. Pride is God's number one enemy.

Once it comes into our heart, it will take over. God will be out and then everything will start collapsing around us. **"Pride comes before destruction, and an arrogant spirit before a fall."** (Proverbs 16:18)

In closing, let us seek humility; humility says, "God must be first in everything!"

47

Super Human Energy!

"For this I labor [unto weariness], striving with all the superhuman energy which He so mightily enkindles and works within me." (Colossians 1:29 AMP)

Have you ever woken up with a deep desire to do something that you had never thought about doing or felt that you previously didn't have the ability to do? Do you ever wonder where that desire came from or what prompted sudden feeling to move forward?

I believe that this kind of stuff happens because God wants to position us for the advancement of His Name upon the earth.

Quickened with God's Idea

Every time that the Lord wants to advance His cause, He will move by His Spirit and quicken our mortal bodies [body, mind and spirit]. The Lord will awaken our faculties and will get our hearts super energized with His idea and purpose.

It doesn't matter if we have never seen it (the idea) before; it doesn't matter whether we understand it or not; know that God wants to reveal to you and use you!

The Lord will empower us or "mightily enkindle" within us and His fire, and will get us flowing in His purpose and plan.

Burnt Out?

One of the things I have noticed in my own walk, is that when I get weary and tired mentally and eventually physically, it is due to the lack of energy. Moving in the flesh has its benefits, but it wears off. This earthly energy eventually runs out of steam.

Many believers are living in this realm. They are tired and burnt out with work, ministry and family. Why is this?

It has been my experience that when I have made decisions based on my own feelings and not upon the emotion of God, I burn out and get frustrated with my own ideas and plans.

Super-Human Energy

The Apostle Paul alludes to this very fact in Colossians 1, when he says that it is God who gives Him this "super-human energy." It is God who imparts this "superhuman energy," and then enkindles it in the human heart.

Let us avail ourselves of this power by simply taking the time to listen in prayer. When God reveals His strategy, along with it, comes this superhuman energy to carry it out! All glory to One who holds all things in His hand.

48

Wherever God Is – Be There!

"Also Amaziah said unto Amos, O thou seer, go, flee thee away into the land of Judah, and there eat bread, and prophesy there: But prophesy not again any more at Beth-el: for it is the king's chapel, and it is the king's court. Then answered Amos, and said to Amaziah, I was no prophet, neither was I a prophet's son; but I was an herdman, and a gatherer of sycamore fruit: And the Lord took me as I followed the flock, and the Lord said unto me, Go, prophesy unto my people Israel." (Amos 7:12-15)

In pursuit of the Lord's will for my own life, I have discovered that the Lord is truly no respecter of persons. Whether you are a man or a woman, or whether you have a career or not, whether you have a high status in society or are dirt poor — God doesn't measure a vessel by these standards.

It is the Lord's desire to make and use a vessel that will carry His will forth on the earth — this I believe is in the center of God's desires.

Let us take for example the servant Amos. In the Scripture noted above, we see Amos prophesying to the king of Israel. Obviously, his prophetic words were not welcomed by anyone in the king's courts, so Amos would be criticized; it was mainly Amaziah the priest who would not allow Amos to prophesy to the king of Israel.

The Calling

Apparently, Amos was already moving in his divine calling in his lot in life. Amos was working as a herdsman and probably supplemented his income by also gathering and selling sycamore fruit.

One can make the argument that perhaps Amos was happy and fulfilled doing his job, after all, it was an honorable thing to do. Working for a living is always a good thing to do!

Yet in all his working, God was ready to take this man to a higher ground. God was about to carry Amos into another realm – the realm of His Spirit, the realm of His will.

I believe every believer must walk responsibly in two areas: First, with his present occupation– and secondly, in hearing God's prophetic word in kairos time, in now time!

Always aspire to be where God needs you to be. Wherever God is – be there!

We never know the hidden potential: The next word from the Lord might change our vocation and alter our destiny.

49

Worrying is Not for You!

"Therefore, I say to you, do not worry about your life, what you will eat or what you will drink; nor about your body, what you will put on. Is not life more than food and the body more than clothing? Look at the birds of the air, for they neither sow nor reap nor gather into barns; yet your heavenly Father feeds them. Are you not of more value than they? Which of you by worrying can add one cubit to his stature?

"So why do you worry about clothing? Consider the lilies of the field, how they grow: they neither toil nor spin; and yet I say to you that even Solomon in all his glory was not arrayed like one of these. Now if God so clothes the grass of the field, which today is, and tomorrow is thrown into the oven, will He not much more clothe you, O you of little faith?

"Therefore, do not worry, saying, 'What shall we eat?' or 'What shall we drink?' or 'What shall we wear?' For after all these things the Gentiles seek. For your heavenly Father knows that you need all these things. But seek first the kingdom of God and His righteousness, and all these things shall be added to you." (Matthew 6:23-33)

While meditating on this subject, I was quickened by the Spirit of God that worrying is truly something that believers have the potential of overcoming every single time. It is amazing to me how we tend to worry about externals and hardly ever internals. Let me explain further...

In my experience of dealing with people in my life and ministry, I have come to understand what people worry so much about and why they worry.

Almost always, worry seems to be active in someone who has not received revelation of what God truly signifies in their lives and/or they are yet to understand the kingdom principle of what it means to be a citizen of the kingdom of God.

I have heard too often people say, "I'm worried about not having enough money to pay the light bill."

Does this sound familiar? Or how about, "I am so overwhelmed, that I might lose my job, and then what am I going to do and how am I going to pay my mortgage?"

Trust me, I know what I am talking about! I've been there once too many times before.

Here is what I have hardly ever heard from believers: "Oh my God, I am so cold and so indifferent with God right now! I need to be touched by God once again because I am afraid that if I don't get a hold of Him, I might die."

Or someone say, "I am so worried about my lack of prayer life, that I need to change my schedule to have the time to meet God in my secret closet!"

Yes, all these requests deal with the spiritual man that lives inside of us who believe.

People tend to worry about what they can see, and hardly ever worry about what they cannot see!

After Jesus tells His disciples not to worry about their lives, or what they would eat, drink, or wear (which by the way, are all external things,) He gives to them the solution.

In essence, Jesus is saying, "Don't worry about the externals. If you are going to be worried about anything in life, then here is what you really should be worried about — worry about seeking God's kingdom first and all His righteousness!"

The Lord figured that if a man or a woman could appropriate themselves of this revelation, that they would never worry about anything external ever again!

50

The Ultimate Passion of the Father!

**"For the earth will be filled
With the knowledge of the glory of the Lord,
As the waters cover the sea."** (Habakkuk 2:14)

What a prophetic word! Actually, it's more than a prophetic word — it's God's heart for the world we live in! In God's heart there exists a restoration of all things; everything created will find its place in God's glory.

As a matter of fact, everything (all creation) was made for it to shine for God, not man or anyone else. Our life was created to express God's glory from the very beginning. It was God's original intent for man to reveal the presence of God in the garden.

Adam and Eve

In the beginning, God's vision was for His creation to express His glory upon the earth. It was God's plan that man would express His nature in the world where they had been placed.

We know the end of that story as it is recorded in Genesis 1 through 3 — man failed in his attempt to fully please the Lord. As the serpent (Satan) moved in with seduction, man bought into the lie of the devil and forfeited all of God's design for them.

The Fall of Man

Since man's fall, all humanity has been seeking for God's glory. The Scripture says that "All have sinned and come short of the glory of God." What this means is that man is born without God's glory. Man was left desolate the day he ate of the forbidden fruit — man now lives without hope in the world.

King Jesus Reigns

"The seventh angel then blew [his] trumpet, and there were mighty voices in heaven, shouting, The dominion (kingdom, sovereignty, rule) of the world has now come into the possession and become the kingdom of our Lord and of His Christ (the Messiah), and He shall reign forever and ever (for the eternity of the eternities)!

Then the twenty-four elders [of the heavenly Sanhedrin], who sit on their thrones before God, prostrated themselves before Him and worshiped, Exclaiming, To You we give thanks, Lord God Omnipotent, [the One] Who is and [ever] was, for assuming the high sovereignty and the great power that are Yours and for beginning to reign." (Revelation 11:15-17)

It was not until Jesus Christ (the glory of the Father) was sent to walk the earth and carry out His mission to redeem the world. Full hope and restoration was all made possible at the cross of Calvary.

Remember, it was through the shed blood at Calvary's

cross that our sins were forgiven; and by His death and resurrection, our flesh was conquered.

Restoration was made possible because the Father had it in His heart that His creation would live forever in His glory. This vision still stands as the ultimate passion in God's heart.

Called to Express His Glory!

Our calling is a sure one! God saved us from darkness with the purpose that we may stand before Him forgiven and be filled with His glory. It is this glory that abides within a forgiven man that speaks to the world.

Let us live on the offense; let us live to express God's glory to the world!

51

Awakened to Act!

"Then the word of the Lord came by Haggai the prophet, saying, 'Is it time for you yourselves to dwell in your paneled houses, and this temple to lie in ruins?' Now therefore, thus says the Lord of hosts: Consider your way! (Haggai 1:3-5)

"Then Zerubbabel-the son of Shealtiel, and Joshua the son of Jehozadak, the high priest, with all the remnant of the people, obeyed the voice of the Lord their God, and the words of Haggai the prophet, as the Lord their God had sent him; and the people feared the presence of the Lord. Then Haggai, the Lord's messenger, spoke the Lord's message to the people, saying, 'I am with you, says the Lord.' So the Lord stirred up the spirit of Zerubbabel, the son of Shealtiel, governor of Judah, and the spirit of Joshua the son of Jehozadak, the high priest, and the spirit of all the remnant of the people; and they came and worked on the house of the Lord of hosts, their God, on the twenty-fourth day of the sixth month, in the second year of King Darius." (Haggai 1:12-15)

Let me share some interesting things I discovered during a moment of silence before the Lord:

God's temple is in ruins, and no one cares! God's house is in reproach, and no one is moved by natural inclination to do anything about it! I mean, why would anyone care? Afterall, its God's people; if they don't care, why would anyone else?

God's People are Moved by His Spirit

The conviction to see, to feel, and to move — did not come without God's Holy Spirit speaking or revealing God's heart to His own people. It took a prophet from the Lord named Haggai to bring forth this convicting word of concern!

The Ability to See

When God speaks to our hearts, it is always with the intent to reveal. God speaks in pictures. He shows a panorama of what is actually happening; He also reveals what He intends to do about the particular situation at hand.

Always remember that when God does speak, it is with the intent to reveal His heart!

The Ability to Feel

Along with the revelation of a clear picture of God's heart, comes God's emotions. To feel what God feels is truly something awesome! Sometimes we hear a word from the Lord, but we fail to capture the emotion. We must always make every effort to get a "feel" for what God is saying to our hearts from His. The timing and the urgency of His heart can all be felt if we are touched by His feelings.

The Ability to Move!

God's revelation is more than just pictures and emotions, let me add. God's revelation is also a blueprint filled with instruction and the power to act! Seeing what God desires to do, will stir us. The word stirred used here means, to awake

.

Once we are awakened to what God desires, we must choose to either do His will or by pass it. It is all up to you and I to carry His vision in the earth.

52

What Is God Really Doing?

We tend to act according to our perception. What we see with our eyes and understand with our mind, this is what we perceive as reality or at least in the eyes of the beholder.

We also tend to treat things according to what we think they are worth. If one's mind only sees things negatively, then it will be very difficult for another to come up with a "positive message" and turn him or her around.

Too often, our lives are dealt with bad situations, where one must rise above the circumstances. It is not an easy thing to overcome situations that are unfavorable much less things we don't understand.

So how does one overcome a situation that is not favorable or at least it wasn't exactly what you were hoping for?

Here are some of the things I have learned over the years.

These are things that have to do more with the understanding of God's will versus our own will. I love to have things my way — I mean, who doesn't?

We all, by nature, love to have complete control of everything we become and everything we do — and we can! It only takes a bit of yielding to God's voice, and if we surrender accordingly, we will be on our way to great success in life.

Let me make mention of one portion of Scripture, and then I will explain what I'm really trying to teach in this meditation. The Scriptures are these:

"When the builders laid the foundation of the temple of the Lord, the priests stood in their apparel with trumpets, and the Levites, the sons of Asaph, with cymbals, to praise the Lord, according to the ordinance of David king of Israel. And they sang responsively, praising and giving thanks to the Lord: 'For He is good,

For His mercy endures forever toward Israel.'
Then all the people shouted with a great shout, when —
they praised the Lord, because the foundation of the
house of the Lord was laid. But many of the priests and
Levites and heads of the fathers' houses, old men who
had seen the first temple, wept with a loud voice when
the foundation of this temple was laid before their eyes.
Yet many shouted aloud for joy, so that the people could
not discern the noise of the shout of joy from the noise
of the weeping of the people, for the people shouted
with a loud shout, and the sound was heard afar off."
(Ezra 3:10-13)

In this story, we find two groups of people. Upon complet-
ing the temple's foundation, one group shouted with joy
and celebration, while the other group wept.   Why was
there shouting and celebration while others wept?

Here's what the Scripture says: **"But many of the priests
and Levites and heads of the fathers' houses, old men
who had seen the first temple, wept with a loud voice**

when the foundation of this temple was laid before their eyes."

There appeared to be a group among God's people who had seen the original temple; this new temple foundation was nothing like the original. I could understand the heartbreak and discontentment. Sometimes in our own lives we don't ever get back to where we were originally, but it doesn't mean that the game is over!

The other group was probably a group of younger servants. They probably had not seen the original temple, thus the celebration and joy of this new one.

We need to have a heart for the new thing but still have our feet grounded on who God is, at all times.

Shifting Times

So, what does it mean when things around us have shifted or changed?

To me, it means an opportunity to see what God desires to bring into fruition in us! Opening our hearts to God's will is key. If we get "stuck in the past," with its idea, philosophy, or mindset — we might never see what God has in store for the coming seasons.

I believe that all of us have been at this place. We all have experienced change this way. It is not fun, it is not joyful in the present moment; nevertheless, God will stretch our faith, our patience, and our knowledge so that we may make it to the end. Thank God for all the changes that await us!

Ministry Information

For more information regarding the ministry of Master-builder Ministries, Inc., preaching engagements, leadership conferences, Vessels Seminars (Leadership Training Seminars,) Masterbuilder School of Ministry or Arise! Leadership School of Leadership - feel free to email Pastor David Mayorga:

david_mayorga@sbcglobal.net

mayorga1126@gmail.com

Also, feel free to check out our website at:
www.masterbuildertx.com

You can locate our ministry base at this address:

Masterbuilder Ministries, Inc.
3833 N. Taylor Rd.
Palmhurst, Texas 78573

Ministry Resources
Other Books by David Mayorga

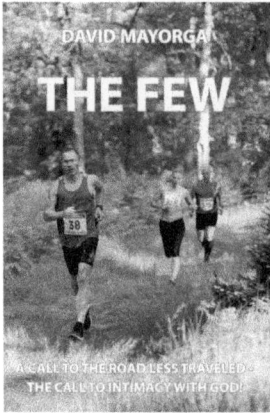

THE FEW
A Call to the Road Less
Traveled-The Call to
Intimacy with God

ISBN - 9780999171004

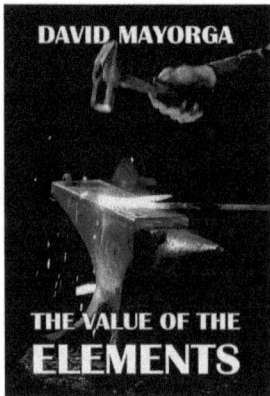

**THE VALUE OF THE
ELEMENTS**

ISBN - 978099917104

All Books Can Be Purchased at:
www.shabarpublications.com

Volume 3

`

The Heart of David Journal

David Mayorga

Volume 3

The Heart of David Journal

David Mayorga

Volume 3

The Heart of David Journal

David Mayorga

Volume 3

www.ingramcontent.com/pod-product-compliance
Lightning Source LLC
Chambersburg PA
CBHW021821090426
42811CB00028B/1935